Introduction

So, here's my book! For years I'... anyone who'll listen about the ... having clarity and order in our ho... aspects of our lives – and, lo and be... ...ncept has caught on! There's now a real ap... ...te for simple living and decluttering: we've woken up to the fact that when it comes to the possessions that surround us, less is so often more.

I'm really excited that my ideas and methods for achieving this way of life are finally all recorded here, in one place, ready to inspire you to declutter and reorganise your home in a way which fits into your busy life. Here are my tried-and-tested techniques for bringing into homes both organisation and, just as importantly, all of the wonderful headspace that comes along with it.

Decluttering is my profession and every day I see the effect it has on people's lives. I also see how each client is different – their home, their lifestyle and their preferences are unique to them. For this reason, my methods are friendly and adaptable, there is no dictating – just a set of principles and helpful tips that you can apply to best suit your space and the way you live your life.

Throughout the book I demonstrate how you don't necessarily need large chunks of time to bring order to your life, a huge amount can be achieved over time if you take twenty minutes here and there. Once you get started you'll find the process so rewarding that it will become infectious.

My techniques are easy and never complicated – complication is so often a barrier when it comes to achieving change. Simplicity is key. I believe that in keeping my methods 'back to basics', they will become second nature to you.

It's not about minimalism and definitely not about creating show-home-style perfection. What I will help you achieve is a friendly level of organisation. Imagine how much easier your hectic days could be if everything you needed was within easy reach, if your clothes were neatly organised in a way that choosing what to wear was a pleasure and your paperwork was stored in such a straightforward way that filing was quick and easy. Picture yourself coming home to a relaxing space where everything has a place. Your home should work *for* you, not against you; it should reduce your stress and anxiety levels, not send them sky high. This process is vital for your wellbeing and you'll very quickly feel the effects – it's truly life-changing. So much more can be achieved in our daily lives if we are operating from a place of calm and order.

Use my book as a go-to guide for reclaiming and enjoying your space. I've set out my methods clearly and made them easy to follow so as to inspire you into action. Happy reading!

Vicky
xxx

1

How It All Started

I've always been an avid tidier and ever since I can remember, sorting and organising drawers, rooms and spaces has made me happy and calm. It's as simple as that.

I have a vivid memory of my eight-year-old self diligently rearranging her bedroom to create what could be described as a miniature bedsit, even down to having a tea and coffee station featuring a real teapot and mug set up on a little desk. A cabin-style bed was top of my Christmas list and I created an area, complete with bowl and bed, for the dog I hoped to get for my birthday. (The dog never appeared ... and neither did the monkey which I was also hoping for.) Arranging my belongings and creating order within a space gave me a sense of peace and, as the youngest of three in a busy family, this was probably the only way I was going to get it.

As the most house-proud member of my family, it was always me who would rush around tidying up before my friends came to play. I would make sure that all the items on show were matching and any odd cutlery or crockery was hidden away. I felt that all my friends had beautiful show-home houses, and while this is not something I would aspire to now, I suppose I believed I had to comply with other families' apparently pristine standards. Order is still vital in my life, I can't function without it, but I now understand that striving for 'perfection' is different – it's an unrealistic, unhealthy goal. For me, the style of show-home living that I used to envy as a child is not worth aspiring to. It's too clinical and hard to maintain for most of us. Have you ever sat down for a cuppa in someone's house only to have the mug whipped away the moment you've taken your last sip? Before you know it, it's been washed and put back in its cupboard. This approach is too extreme – for the guest it's unrelaxing and for the host suggests a nervous preoccupation with immaculate living that must be exhausting and unhealthy to sustain. Instead I now aim for 'friendly levels of organisation', a phrase that I'll use throughout this book. It means not panicking when something is out of place for a second – every day is full of moments of disorder, but that's OK, these moments are temporary. It's about accepting small windows of chaos in the happy knowledge that systems are in place to make restoring order quick and easy.

When I left school (unaware that my passion for organising could become a valid profession!) I trained to be a nanny. I'd always loved children so this seemed a sensible option. Looking back, this was the first of several roles that have each, in different ways, shaped my belief that simple, organised living is not just possible for all of us, it's essential for our wellbeing.

At the age of eighteen, working for a family looking after their four young children, I soon realised that organisation was the key to survival. Relatively small tasks like sorting the children's clothes so that they were in order and to hand, or storing toys so they were easy for little hands to reach and just as easy to tidy away, made a huge difference to the smooth running of the day and meant we had more time for fun activities. And the bigger challenges could be met if the systems were in place at home for organised living. I loved tackling the children's bedrooms and playrooms – my nanny training and growing experience with the kids gave me a basic insight into child psychology and I soon came to realise that they need headspace as much as adults do – this is something that shapes my beliefs and the way I work to this day.

Looking after the four little ones was fun but hectic and when the role came to a natural end I took up some bar and reception work at a local golf club. Soon afterwards, I was approached by a golf management company about becoming a PA. I seized the chance although, in truth, I had no idea what a PA was – this was before we looked everything up on Google! – but I was about to find out . . . I spent the next four years travelling the world as a PA for professional golfers; my desk was anything from a restaurant table to a departure lounge floor to a balcony overlooking a golf course. It was an amazing time which required organisation on a whole new level! After the golfers came my role as PA for twenty-five professional footballers. This was an office-based job and, after two years behind a desk with them, I made up my mind what my next role should involve. My wish list was to travel, to work for one person and to learn about a new industry.

My wishes were granted when I became PA to Lily Allen. This exciting chapter of my life brought with it a host of new experiences and skills. Supporting Lily and making all her personal arrangements for an eighteen-month tour which took in Australia, Europe, Japan and the States involved incredibly detailed planning. Once again my desk was a dressing-room floor, a seat in a tour bus . . . basically anywhere I could get Wi-Fi. We would always need several bags packed – for a hotel stay, a flight, a social engagement, a gig or a night on the tour bus – but I still had to be able to lay my hands on any item at a moment's notice, from a couple of hairpins to an outfit from Lily's tour wardrobe. I thrived on these daily challenges; the smallest details made such a big difference to our day running smoothly. While on the tour I would have the occasional day back at home in the UK when I might have twenty-four hours to turn everything around, sort any home admin, wash and repack. Those were hectic, unbelievable and unforget-table days! I had to meticulously organise my own life as well as Lily's, and having a place of calm and order as my base was crucial to my wellbeing.

Life as a PA meant making big things happen, from booking exotic holidays to sorting the logistics of house moves, yet over the years I was struck by how the organisational tasks I completed in clients' homes, like a wardrobe detox or simply tidying up a messy drawer, seemed to bring them such happiness. These small touches prompted so much gratitude, and I noted how making these tweaks in people's homes impacted positively on their day-to-day lives, giving them a real energy boost. So, when it was time for my wonderful adventure with Lily to come to an end, I knew where my future lay – in helping people improve all aspects of their life by bringing calm and order to their homes. 'Professional organiser' was never on my school's career list and yet – after years working in other industries – it now feels like the most natural choice. I spend my days giving clients back their headspace by bringing order into their homes. For me this is the most satisfying, fulfilling job possible!

On tour with Lily, her booking agent used to joke with anyone who came into the dressing room looking stressed – he'd put his hand on their shoulder and say, 'You need a Vicky!' So when it came to naming my new business this comment was the obvious choice – a little cheesy maybe, but catchy and memorable, and it always makes me smile.

I was (and still am!) so excited at the prospect of working with clients in their homes, but in the early days I found that some people didn't share my enthusiasm and clearly didn't understand what a professional organiser did ... or perhaps thought that the idea just wouldn't catch on. When I explained what I did for a living, I got used to confused responses from those who clearly thought the whole idea was very strange. I called them the 'head tilters' and can see them now, heads to the side, smiling and saying, 'Well, good luck with *that* ...' It was great to bump into the same people later and to be able to tell them that actually it was going amazingly – I was soon fully booked weeks in advance and could barely keep up with demand!

One of my first bookings was to reorganise the wardrobe of the founder of Storm modelling agency, Sarah Doukas, which was an amazing confidence boost. Here was an incredibly successful and talented lady, with a black book bursting with people she could have called on to help her with the task – but she chose me! The reality was that, despite having so many contacts in the world of fashion, *I* was the person Sarah wanted for the job. This cemented in my mind that there was a definite gap in the market for You Need A Vicky, *Professional Organiser.*

I'd fallen into working as a PA, but once I landed the role I had made it my mission to be the best PA out there and my determination was just as great in my new role as professional organiser – I felt passionately that I was going to take this to another level, to lead the field. In my personal life I'm not competitive but when it comes to my business it's different, I feel driven to be the best. A year after setting up I had a steady stream of clients, business was going well and I noticed a change in many people's perception of my work. There has been a gradual shift in understanding about how clutter affects our life, coupled with a deeper understanding of mental wellbeing – and the two are inextricably linked. I would find myself holding a whole table's interest at weddings when it came to my turn to explain what I did. I didn't have a baby or a husband to talk about, but increasingly my line of work was provoking interest and intrigue; everyone could relate to it in some way and people often asked for advice on tackling their own wardrobe, paperwork or playroom.

However, I also soon noticed a presumption among those I spoke to that my clients were hoarders and I was always quick to tell them this was not the case. Hoarding was recognised as a mental disorder in 2015 and requires specialist help, usually from those with a background in psychology. My methods are not tailored to the approaches that hoarders require, and neither is this book. (It's really important to encourage a hoarder to seek the right help, so if you or anyone you know needs help with hoarding, please see the references on page 197 for links for help and advice.) I see my job as helping ordinary people take back control of their lives and headspace – people who have let the amount of 'stuff' in their homes take over and start to damage their ability to live happily. And that's what this book will help you to do too.

As people became more aware of the benefits of living with less, my bookings increased and at times in my second year of business I had a three-month waiting list. Word was spreading about my methods and it was so gratifying to be in such demand. My techniques are based on experiences: every method has been tried and tested and has a specific memory attached, often from several years ago. On tour with Lily, the drawers of her tour wardrobe were deep, so it made sense to pack everything vertically, meaning it could all be seen at a glance; when looking after my little nephew, I panicked when he pulled a heavy toy down on himself from a high shelf, narrowly avoiding injury. Life was, and still is, a series of experiences to learn simple lessons from. When starting the business I made a conscious decision not to read any books on decluttering or organising – something I still keep to, as I don't want to cloud my mind with other theories when I have tried and tested my own methods and know that they work.

My clients are a wonderful mix of people with a huge range of lifestyles, and that keeps my bookings varied and exciting. I work with busy families, businessmen and women, those who travel a lot or are embarking on a new chapter in life such as a new job, a house move or first child, as well as sports personalities and celebrities. Working with those who face significant challenges such as bereavement or issues like anxiety is also an important part of what I do. Helping people restore control and stability and to see their home as a sanctuary of calm is a privilege, and can make an enormous difference to someone's life. I know how much I rely on my own home to level me and keep me grounded in times of chaos.

By following the methods in my book you can make a huge difference to the way you live – I'll even be breaking everything down into manageable chunks to make it easy for you. It might sound like a dramatic claim, but I know from experience how creating order at home can impact positively on *every* part of your world. Operating from a place of calm and living with organisation will affect your state of mind, your work, your relationships, family life, your ability to make decisions, your energy levels and your confidence. The fact that you've picked up this book means that you are open to the benefits my friendly level of organisation will bring. You've taken the first step and I promise you the process is more achievable and enjoyable than you anticipate – it's a life-enhancing journey, not a chore.

Let's get started; I have a feeling you'll love it!

2

Simple Living

At the end of the day, being organised is about having more time for yourself, and enabling you to live a more balanced life.

Dr Eva Selhub, M.D., *Your Health Destiny: How to Unlock Your Natural Ability to Overcome Illness, Feel Better, and Live Longer* (2015)

I couldn't agree more!

Simple Living is how I describe the organised, uncluttered lifestyle I enjoy and that I believe you will too. We are overwhelmed with choices in so many areas of our lives and making one decision after another takes up headspace. This is why I like to keep things simple at home.

Imagine that you are you eating out at a lovely restaurant, one where the menu goes on for pages and pages. Everything looks delicious, but you feel overwhelmed and paralysed by choice. Personally, I find it so much easier to make a decision when there are fewer dishes on offer. This theory applies to scenarios throughout your home: picture your wardrobe, your toiletries, your child's mass of toys … often there is simply *too much to choose from.*

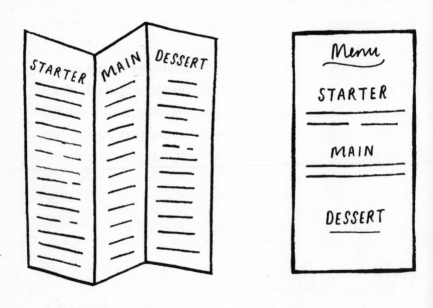

There is no need to have cupboards bursting with cups and cutlery, bathrooms clogged with an endless array of products and wardrobes crowded with more outfits than we have time to wear. By clearing space and taking away unnecessary choices we can make our days more streamlined and cut out some of the decisions we are faced with. Instead of having a rail full of tops to choose from in the morning, I've cut mine down to only those that I *know* I wear and feel great in. When it comes to beauty products, I only ever have one shampoo, face cream and body lotion on the go at once; they are all from ranges I love so there's no need for a wide selection and, best of all, there is no choice involved. The same goes for crockery, stationery, cleaning products and many, many more possessions – the key is keeping it simple. And, by simplifying small areas of your home, you wouldn't believe the overall space you will be creating.

Panic buying – prompted by anything be it a severe weather forecast, a bank-holiday break, or special offer – often leads us to stockpile products, especially food. We stash away tins and packets believing that having our cupboards full to bursting will afford us some security or save us some money. But, more often than not, the downside of buying in bulk outweighs any gain. The cumulative effect of having crowded spaces, overflowing storage and trying to race against the calendar to eat food before its use-by date is a feeling of pressure, of being overwhelmed.

When our lives seem out of control, we tend to understand that it's important to take charge and bring order where we can. This can mean saying 'no' to invitations or limiting our commitments – we start protecting our time. But keeping areas clear and organised in our homes is just as important as managing our diary in this way. Most elements of our life could benefit from a degree of simplification. When we are up to date with our paperwork, work surfaces are free from clutter and we have regained control at home, we operate from a position of clarity. The simplicity we begin to enjoy at home can spill over into all areas of our lives, giving us confidence and impacting on how we manage ourselves socially and professionally.

By following my methods, Simple Living can be achieved easily and within the context of a busy life. Once it becomes a habit, you'll learn to regard material possessions differently. You will become more selective about what you allow to come into and stay in your home, and you will limit the choices you need to make each day by letting go of the items that are cluttering up your spaces. When you have simplified small areas of your home and brought order to your cupboards and storage, you won't believe the overall space you will be creating and the feeling of calm that will result.

Decluttering and wellbeing

Simple Living has a direct relationship to wellbeing and mindfulness, two concepts we now hear about regularly. Mindfulness is a state of active, open attention to the present. When you're mindful, you observe your thoughts and feelings from a distance, you let them drift in and out without judging them. Mindfulness means truly *living in the moment*, and it seems that more and more of us are taking the time (and it only takes a moment) to allow ourselves this experience and truly live in the 'now'.

Yet, while we increasingly understand the importance of being mindful and that if our heads are too full our wellbeing will suffer, we are often so bogged down by clutter that we don't feel able to make positive changes. When I feel stressed or anxious I take a step back to 'reset' myself, but this doesn't work if the first thing I see when I re-engage with my surroundings is untidiness and disarray. In the same way, if we take time out for yoga or to meditate but then open our eyes to a home which is out of control, the benefits of our mindful practices quickly evaporate. No matter how relaxed we may have felt, being confronted by chaos, to-do lists and piles of mail to sort through can reverse the effects and mean we quickly revert to our 'stressed out' state. But coming home to a place of order and simplicity can do wonders for our frame of mind. Calm surroundings breed calm minds – it just makes sense.

Simple, streamlined living also means we are more likely to follow a healthy diet, or stick to routines. Clutter around us sends our minds and senses into overdrive; it distracts us from the task in hand, reminds us of unfinished jobs, makes us feel inadequate because we haven't organised ourselves, and prevents us from relaxing – all of this is stressful for the brain. Stress means you're more likely to resort to coping mechanisms such as reaching for comfort foods or the TV remote than if you spend time in calm, ordered surroundings.

Stress doesn't just stem from unfiled paperwork or general clutter around the home, it also comes from abandoned projects. Having half-finished tasks hanging over you, like a craft project, or an unopened healthy-eating book, makes us feel guilty that we haven't had a chance or made the time to complete them, and seeing them lying around (or even just knowing that they are stashed away under the stairs) adds to the feeling of pressure on our time, when often there simply aren't enough hours in the day to pursue these interests. On declutter days, I ask clients to be realistic about whether they are ever likely to finish these little ventures. Why not give yourself a fresh start and free yourself from any abandoned projects you have around the house? And be wary then of taking on any more projects that you might not have time for. One study by psychologists in America found that women who described their homes as 'cluttered' or full of 'unfinished projects' were more likely to be depressed or tired and to have higher levels of the stress hormone cortisol than those who felt their homes had a 'restful' and 'restorative' feel.

If you need any further convincing, research in America has shown that having a tidy, clutter-free bedroom will help you get a better night's sleep, which ultimately impacts on your mood, performance at work and mental health. The study, conducted by New York's St Lawrence University, found that people who have more stuff filling the open space in their bedrooms take longer to nod off than those with neat and organised rooms.

There is plenty of proof out there that simple, organised living benefits all aspects of our lives – our sleep, health, wellbeing – but do we really need studies to tell us this? It's common sense really, and I've seen first-hand the amazing impact that streamlining your home can have.

Although work was crazy I felt in control when I was there, but in the evenings I just couldn't relax at home. The clutter around my flat was stopping me from being able to wind down after a day at work. I had too much 'stuff' and my home had stopped being a special place for me to switch off. I cannot believe the difference that Vicky has made. I love coming home and feeling the benefit that this space has given me. For me, it's not a choice, it's a necessity.

Leah, 29

It's rare to meet someone these days who doesn't feel that their life is too busy and that they simply have 'too much on'. Creating order at home is a great step in helping us all gain back control of our lives. The positive impact that this kind of 'home therapy' can provide is powerful, and I know I'm not being over-dramatic in saying so; I've seen it happen so many times that I'm confident it really will change the way you live.

To have or to be?

I'm no science boffin, but I am a *big* fan of US crime shows and every now and then I actually learn something from tuning in. (I can totally justify my TV habit – it's educational!) It was my love of *CSI* that brought the German psychologist and psychoanalyst Erich Fromm (1900–80) into my life, his insight into our consumerist culture really helped me clarify and shape my own ideas about how we live with our belongings. In an episode called 'House of Hoarders' I saw about five years ago, one of the show's lead characters, Raymond Langston (played by Laurence Fishburne), describes the thinker's beliefs:

> ❝ Erich Fromm forecast a society obsessed with possessions. People have two basic orientations – Having and Being. A person with a Having orientation desires to possess things, property, even people, but a person with a Being orientation focusses on the experience, they derive meaning from exchanging, engaging and sharing with other people ... unfortunately Fromm also predicted that a culture driven by consumerism, like the one we live in today, is doomed to the 'having' orientation, which leads to dissatisfaction and emptiness. ❞

Langston then points out that while possessions shouldn't come to mean *everything*, they also don't have to be devoid of meaning – they are one of the ways that we experience and enjoy life – it's about making sure our possessions don't get in the way of living. It's all about *balance*.

Those words really struck a chord with me as I considered how many of us are surrounded by objects and belongings that are getting in the way of living. After all, this desire to free people from the material baggage that weighs them down is what motivates me to go to work every day! However sceptical my clients are initially, they inevitably surprise themselves at how freedom from the possessions they once thought they couldn't live without enhances their lives. I often get calls or messages from people I've worked with, telling me that they really aren't missing the box-loads of 'stuff' that I encouraged them to part with after all, and in fact they've since continued to declutter and are embracing living with less. For me that feedback is the best buzz of all. The space that I give back to clients is mental as much as physical; it allows them to prioritise experience over possessions and to get on with the joy of living ... and I mean really *living*, not just existing day to day.

Up until the 1990s, self-storage sites were unheard of in the UK and yet now there are more than 1,000 across the country providing over thirty million square feet of storage – enough to fill Wembley Stadium around twenty-five times! This represents a *crazy* amount of clutter. Instead of re-evaluating what we really need and what makes us feel genuinely happy, we are just boxing up and hiding away belongings that don't fit in our houses.

I think it's fair to say that as a society, we have become preoccupied with 'having' and with using our belongings to define our identities. But things are beginning to change. While the rise in public storage sites has rocketed in the last decades, there has also been a growing discomfort within society over the consequences of our materialism and consumption. The environmental and social impacts of intensive farming and mass-manufacturing niggle at our conscience and increasingly we are beginning to look beyond price tags to the story behind products on the shelves. Do we really *need* or even *want* them? Taking responsibility for our choices as consumers leads us to question all of our buying decisions and, aside from the ethical issues that a purchase might throw up, we also come to realise that this compulsive need to shop, the buzz of a bargain, does not guarantee contentment. If it is not the clutter on our shelves, then what does make us happy? Perhaps it's an age thing, but I'm sure most of us reach a point where we realise that accumulating a mass of material objects does not bring us happiness – in fact, sometimes quite the opposite. Our lives should be about our time and how we spend it, not about the possessions we gather along the way. I hope that we are beginning to realise that it's the journey, the experiences, sharing time with others, being productive and rising to challenges that give us the biggest boost of happy hormones.

Controlling the flow of what enters our homes

The drive for a quick fix often leads us to make another online purchase, or to grab another top from the sale rail, but the truth is that any buzz we get from our new purchase is likely to short-lived. We later find our homes crowded with possessions and this can leave us feeling not only guilty about unworn clothes and unused gadgets, but desperate for physical and mental space.

I am strict about what I buy and keep at home, but for me this isn't an effort – it's a natural process which helps me keep order and calm. By following my methods you too will find yourself becoming selective about what is allowed into your home and, most importantly, what stays.

You will probably find your stress levels rising at certain times of year (particularly Christmas and birthdays, if you have children) when the flood of objects coming into your home can seem out of control. This comment from one of my clients echoes the sentiments of so many mums that I have worked with:

When I see guests arriving at my children's parties, clutching presents, I'm just full of dread. I feel like such an old misery when I know it should be a happy time, but all I'm thinking is *where on earth am I going to put it all?* Both children already have so much, it's stressful. I feel ungrateful, but the kids just don't need any more.

Alex, 38

Such occasions are the perfect time to practise a little Simple Living. If friends and family ask what you or your children would like as gifts, be armed and ready with a list of items that you or they *actually need*. Obviously not everyone will ask, but by being prepared with suggestions (and perhaps some of these could be vouchers/experiences) you have some control over the influx of clutter – sorry, I mean gifts! – that will be coming your way. And practise what you preach: instead of trawling online for present ideas or traipsing up and down the High Street, consider that maybe, if no obvious present springs to mind, the recipient does not actually need or want for anything. Instead of giving a physical object, why not share a special experience together? Make a memory instead of giving the gift of clutter!

Why can't we let go?

Later on, I'll explore in more depth the most common reasons that many of us have for hanging on to so many possessions. In my experience these usually fall into five categories:

Sentiment

Guilt

Lack of time to tackle the piles of 'stuff'

Fear that sorting through belongings will be
a stressful task

Uncertainty over where to start

You will probably be able to place yourself in one
or more of these categories – and in the chapters that
follow I will set out the best ways of clearing your clutter
and bringing a friendly level of organisation into your
life, whatever reason you have for having collected too
much in your home. This will help you to think more
clearly and exist more freely – a more streamlined way
of living is within your grasp! My advice also applies to
those who describe themselves as 'messy'; people who
believe it's an inherent personality trait that cannot be
changed and that order and organisation will always
be out of their reach. I have had many clients over the
last six years who have changed the way they thought
they inherently were by following my advice and prac-
tising straightforward methods. Nothing I suggest is
complicated, it's all about going back to basics, and the
solutions are maintainable. Complex systems go out of
the window – if you have to think about how to do it,
then it just won't work!

My belief in Simple Living should not be confused
with minimalism or creating clinical, show-home-style
spaces. It's about freeing our homes from unwanted,
unnecessary clutter and reassessing what belongings
we *really* want to surround ourselves with and how we
organise them to best suit our lives.

3

Letting Go

It's a great privilege to be invited into someone's home. Over the years I have heard so many explanations, often very personal, as to why our homes can become overcrowded with belongings that we no longer want or need – and for every reason we have for hanging on to these objects, I have a method to help you move them on and free up your space, helping you to let go.

Sentimental attachments

The problem: *I inherited it*

> *The chair's not really my style and I haven't actually got anywhere to put it, but I can't get rid of it because my aunt left it to me in her will*

So often a client will explain the presence of a random piece of furniture or ornament in their home by detailing how it was handed down to them, given by, or inherited from a much-loved relative. We often feel obliged to hold on to such pieces, including clothes and knick-knacks, and believe that we could not bear to be parted from them. We can find ourselves filling cupboards, boxes and lofts with a whole host of possessions that won't ever see the light of day again because they do not suit our tastes – and yet we feel that we must keep them. Don't get me wrong, I'm not suggesting that you have a ruthless cull of everything that you inherit. Many of us have a few treasured items, often photos or jewellery, that we love having on display or wearing; they bring back happy memories, suit our style and are a positive presence in our lives. These belongings are not the problem – what I'm talking about is the cupboard-hogging, space-stealing 'stuff' that is crowding corners and dragging us down.

Simple steps to a solution

When I lost my mum three years ago I knew that going through her possessions would be a hard task, but for me it was better faced sooner rather than later. I knew that the longer I left it, the harder I would find it to part with her possessions. To break down the task of dealing with this mountain of belongings, I mentally put each item into one of three categories:

Objects that I genuinely loved and would treasure.

Items I would feel guilty about parting with but didn't feel a huge attachment to.

Belongings that I felt little attachment to and could easily part with.

It would have been so easy to hang on to those items in the middle category, but deep down I knew this wasn't the solution. Instead, I asked myself the questions detailed below and acted immediately on my responses. Try doing the same with any inherited belongings you are unsure of, being mindful to focus fond thoughts and memories specifically on those items you truly love rather than automatically attaching sentimental value to every item. If you are doing this with a lot of belongings, as you go through the questions below, pop Post-it notes on everything you are planning on keeping. This will help you to visualise how much you need to find space for. If the room becomes a sea of little yellow squares, then you need to rethink some choices!

1. Is it my taste?

If you saw this object on sale, would you consider buying it? If the answer is 'no' and you cannot honestly see a place for the possession in your home, then it's time to let it go. Our homes reflect our personalities, they are our sanctuary, and it is vital that we feel 'at home' in our own spaces. If the happiness an object brings you doesn't outweigh the unease you feel about how it looks in your home, then the decision is made! Filling rooms with objects which aren't our personal choice can stop us from enjoying our surroundings. If you have inherited an item of value that you really do not see belonging in your home, why not sell it and use the money towards an object or experience that has a meaningful connection with your lost loved one?

A client of mine inherited, from her mother, a large distinctive antique table which she admitted she really didn't like the look of – she was actually beginning to resent it for the space it was taking up. She found herself justifying to guests that the table wasn't her choice and that she didn't like it. I suggested that she overcame her guilt, parted with it and spent the money on an experience dedicated to her mum. We talked about her mother's passion for music, so I suggested she used the proceeds to take the family on a trip to a musical. She was delighted at this suggestion. It was a lovely way of keeping her mother's passion and her memory alive. We shouldn't be turning our noses up at furniture within our own homes: it's a negative reaction to something that belonged to a loved one when our associations with that person should be positive.

2. Do I have the space for it?

This is usually the easiest question to answer. If the grand piano you inherited from your uncle will not fit in your flat then the decision is straightforward. But just because we *do* have the space to store or display possessions we have been given, this does not mean we are obliged to hang on to them. Giving up space for pieces of furniture or boxes of knick-knacks is likely to mean making a sacrifice in another area – it can restrict the amount of room children have to play in, make it harder to access or appreciate other belongings, or simply give the feeling of an area being cluttered. We are often inclined to fill all available spaces, yet allowing some areas to remain clear and open can be important for our wellbeing.

3. Am I going to use it?

Unless we are just about to leave home or move, we rarely inherit items that we *need*. Most of us have already carefully kitted out our homes with the furniture and essentials that we love. This means that to answer this question we must be completely honest with ourselves about whether an item will be of use, and if we don't love it for its appearance then it will need to justify its presence by being extremely useful.

Occasionally, we inherit something lovely – a bookcase, for example – which is far more special than the budget version we bought years ago. In this situation, the inheritance is a real blessing – just make sure you pass on the old shelves and don't keep both! But if you cannot envisage yourself making use of an object, why not pass it on? Note the wise words of the social activist and designer, William Morris:

> ❛ If you want a golden rule that will fit everything, this is it: Have nothing in your houses that you do not know to be useful or believe to be beautiful. ❜

This quote is bandied about so much, but there's a reason for that – it makes perfect sense!

4. Could someone else get more enjoyment than me from this?

When I looked through my mum's clothes, jewellery and treasured pieces, I thought about which items she would have wanted me to pass on to someone else. She believed, and so do I, that belongings are to be enjoyed, not stored away for years. I considered which of her things could be given a whole new life and make someone else happier. I felt I had a natural bond to almost everything – of course I did, these were my mum's possessions and I loved her dearly. But I also knew that she would have told me not to be 'so silly' if I had tried to keep everything I was sorting through. Instead she would have encouraged me to let someone else enjoy it, and that's exactly what I did. As Dad and I unloaded bags and bags at the charity shop (we chose an animal charity that Mum supported) I said to him how proud Mum would be, he agreed ... and we both had another weep. I knew the longer we left this part, the harder it would have been. For me, postponing the process would have only meant putting off the inevitable and having the task hanging over me.

So, when you look through a box of Granny's clothes, think how much she treasured many of these items and how someone else could enjoy them too. Imagine the scenario where a hard-up student walks into a charity shop and her face lights up at an old duffel coat – so old it's now retro. For a few pounds, going to a good cause, the student has nabbed a bargain to suit her vintage look. The coat is once again bringing happiness; it could be given another twenty years of love! The other scenario is that it stays, along with the rest of Granny's wardrobe, in a box, forgotten in the dark, gradually being eaten away by moths for you to guiltily come across every few years and eventually throw away. If you have an entire collection of someone else's belongings to sort through, including clothes, choose a couple of pieces that make you smile and give the rest a whole new life by letting them go.

5. Is the memory a positive one?

The point about memories being positive or negative is key – I'm often surprised how people hold on to the belongings of loved ones when the feelings that these objects provoke can be so sad. When I asked a client about a vase on her shelf she said: 'When I look at that vase I remember how we always kept it filled with fresh flowers by my mum's bed when she was ill. It was such a horrid time.' Every time this lovely lady caught sight of the vase, she recalled her mother's last days and this instantly affected her mood. Instead of remembering a lifetime of laughter and adventure with her mum, this object triggered memories of a traumatic time.

Sometimes we know deep down what we *should* do, but need permission from someone to help us become more decisive. Having a friend to talk the process through with can help – or even just reminding yourself that the feelings you are having are normal. One thing is for sure, passing on an item from a loved one who is no longer around is not severing any emotional link with them. You are separating yourself from a physical object, not from that person. Sometimes our desire to hang on to an object is about needing a trigger for the memory it stirs, rather than valuing the item itself. If you are reluctant to part with something because of the happy memory associated with it, then take a picture of the possession – by having the photograph you will still have something to spark that memory. Later on I'll talk about Memory Boxes, which are the perfect places to store photos like this.

To recap:

Keep *only* the objects that you genuinely love and that you feel have a place in your home.

For possessions that you feel guilty about parting with, but which you do not feel have a place in your home, ask yourself: Is it my taste? Do I actually like it? Do I have the space for this? Am I going to use it? Could someone else get more enjoyment from this?

I know how hard letting go of the possessions of loved ones can be and how we can attach powerful emotions to belongings, but if we do not have the physical space for these objects (and they are just *objects*), if they do not fit within our home or lifestyle and if the memories we associate with them are not positive, it is time to move them on. Our attachments to loved ones are in our hearts and our heads, and bringing calm and organisation to your home will help give you the space and clarity you need to enjoy memories while moving forward. It's OK to let go.

Guilt from spending

The problem: I spent my hard-earned money on that!

> *I'd better hang on to that, I don't use it but I spent good money on it and so it would be a waste to get rid*

When it comes to letting go of belongings, I find that people feel conflicted because they dwell on how much they spent on a particular item. So often I see people making the case for hanging on to something they never use purely because of how much it cost them in the first place. I can almost see their thought process as they dither over a possession: *I'd feel guilty if I got rid of this, it's still got the tags on. I'll just make sure I start using it.* We all feel disappointed in ourselves if we think we may have been frivolous or wasteful, and we try to justify the purchase by convincing ourselves that *one day* it will be useful. I'm not just talking about big expensive items – having anything around that we bought new and yet don't use is enough to prick at our conscience.

Simple steps to a solution

In order to part with belongings and to enjoy the feeling of space that you can create, you need to accept guilt as part of the solution, but not linger on it. Either on a conscious or subconscious level this guilt will have been a cloud that has been hovering over you, getting darker and heavier as you dwell on money that has been wasted. The process that follows will help you become mindful about future spending, as you become more selective about the items that you want in your home. Imagine your home as a giant box: think of the amount of clutter that goes into that box every week and think about the amount that actually leaves. The box that you are imagining is probably overflowing by now, right? The quantity of clutter that we allow into our homes is usually far greater than the number of possessions we move on. We are filling up our homes and the space around us at a faster rate than we realise. Have a little think about how much came through your front door even in the last week? And how much went out . . .

1. Accept that today you have permission to feel guilty and then gather together the belongings that you no longer use . . . or have never used. Now is the moment to acknowledge the guilt, but don't worry – tomorrow it will be gone and you'll have swapped it for headspace as well as physical space. You're going to let it go. So, put what you've gathered to the side and appreciate the space you have created by removing these objects.

The next day, concentrate on the feeling of space and clarity and let the enjoyment you experience from parting with unwanted possessions overcome the guilt that was plaguing you yesterday. Once we begin to realise that living with less is liberating, the process becomes much easier.

2. Move items on *quickly*; don't leave them festering in a bag by the front door. Prioritise removing these possessions from your house as soon as possible. Re-gifting things definitely helps lift the guilt of the money you may have spent on them – and you don't have to wait until someone's birthday or Christmas to give them a present. By sharing the love you can give up the guilt! Or let the objects that have been cluttering up your cupboards fill the shelves of a charity shop. Put them in the boot of your car or by your front door ready to go.

3. Be selective when it comes to what you are going to sell on. You know how much spare time you have, and although some of us relish the process of selling through online auction sites, the truth is that for many of us our good intentions will go to waste and we will be staring at a collection of clutter in a 'to sell' pile for the next year or so. Be realistic: you know yourself better than anyone. This process is about streamlining your life and reducing your to-do list, not adding to it. It's worth asking yourself, if you're intending to sell objects online, how much you consider your time to be worth. Factor in the time that will be spent uploading photos and details, answering queries, packaging the item and queuing in the post office . . . is it really worth it?

4. Clients often tell me that once they've sorted through their belongings and removed mis-buys from their homes, their shopping habits change naturally. They find themselves shopping smarter to avoid the same mistakes happening again. If you are browsing online, allow yourself to add items to your basket – it's the modern way to window shop! – but, before you click 'buy', shut down the window, walk away and distract yourself with something else. See how great it feels. If any of the potential purchases were essential or really important to you, then maybe you will go back and finalise the purchase, but the chances are that, after a short period of time, you will be glad that you didn't. It's a more mindful way to shop and helps us avoid splashing out on spends that are just an impulse or an extravagance. Enjoy the feeling of money that you have saved by not clicking 'buy'!

If you pick up an item in a shop, especially clothing, hold on to it and continue to browse. I do this a lot and, more often than not, I end up putting it back and walking away. Resisting an unnecessary spend can make us feel better than making the purchase itself. Limiting our urge to buy also means that when we do genuinely need something, shopping becomes a rare treat and a process we enjoy taking time over.

To recap:

Identify belongings that you have bought but rarely or never used and place them all in a box/bag. Accept the guilt attached to the money wasted.

Wake up the next day and enjoy the space you've created. With the guilt gone you can concentrate on the positive result you've achieved.

Remove the belongings from your house as quickly as possible – ideally on the same day.

To avoid future mis-buys never shop in a rush and try to walk away from online or in-store purchases before committing to buy.

Keeping it just in case

The problem: This may come in handy one day ...

I felt that I needed to keep so many mugs just in case I had a lot of people over at the same time and everyone wanted a hot drink. Vicky asked me the last time this situation had occurred – of course I instantly realised that it hadn't and wasn't very likely to! I immediately put twenty mugs in the charity pile and laughed at myself!

Abigail, 43

Will it? *Really?* Many of us have possessions that we are convinced will one day spring into use. Boxes of cables, leads and chargers are popular culprits – I have lost count of the number I have come across gathering dust and taking up space in clients' houses. The truth is that most of the cables in these boxes are out of date and no longer compatible with any of the household's appliances. And how many of us have cupboards full of extra glasses or crockery (in case we throw a huge party), extra coats and wellies in random sizes (in case visitors need to borrow them), piles of catalogues that have arrived in the post (in case we have time to read them), cardboard boxes and empty toilet rolls (in case they are needed for craft projects) . . . and so on and so forth. As we sort through our things, how can we decide what we really should hang on to 'just in case'?

Simple steps to a solution

1. Consider who you are keeping the item for and be wary of holding on to belongings in case friends or family members need them. Many mothers will hoard masses of their children's clothing or toys ready to pass on to much younger nieces, nephews or friends' little ones. Try not to fall into the trap of using your home as a holding area for items for other people. Instead, as soon as clothes, toys or equipment are of no use to you, immediately pass them on to the chosen friend or relative so it is then up to them to store them until they are needed. If they genuinely haven't got the space, then make sure they have seen the items you have in mind and that they actually want or need them, as otherwise you will run the risk of storing belongings that are not to their taste or that they wouldn't want anyway. If you are storing boxes for others make sure a time length is agreed after which the items will be handed over.

2. Weigh up the cost of the items versus the inconvenience caused by storing them for long periods of time.

Cables are a good example: instead of using up valuable storage space with a large box or bag of leads that haven't been used for years, ask yourself – in the unlikely event that you were to need one of these cables – how much would it cost to buy a new one? The chances are it will only be a few pounds. Would it be better to bite the bullet and remove the whole box, freeing up some wonderful, much-needed space, while accepting that at some point you may (but more likely may not) have to fork out a few pounds to replace a cable? Measure up the value of enjoying the space and clearing clutter against the worth of the objects. This is especially true of large items such as plastic toys, cushions, extra duvets and sports equipment.

3. Be realistic about keeping items as 'spares'. I often see homes with far more bedding than they could ever need and spare duvets and pillows, which, in particular, are bulky and difficult to store. If you try to cater for every situation where you might have multiple guests sleeping on your sofas or on inflatable beds, your cupboards will soon overflow. Weigh up how often this actually happens. Are you filling up your precious space for an occasion that only happens once a year, if that?

4. Why not hire items instead of buying and then having to store them? Many 'just in case' items are actually available to hire, so instead of forking out for something that you will rarely or perhaps never use, consider whether or not hiring it when it's needed might be more practical. Perhaps you bought a gazebo just in case you had a summer party, or a carpet-cleaning machine just in case you had a stain that wouldn't budge – these are bulky piece of kit which take up valuable space. Before making a 'just in case' purchase, think where you will store it.

I had a client who threw a big party for her husband's fiftieth birthday. She bought hundreds of pieces of plastic tablewear which she then kept afterwards 'just in case'. The plates and glasses took up shelves' worth of space in her garage for the next five years! She even told me she knew she could have hired the tableware for less than she paid for it. If you have friends or family who regularly host big celebrations, then share the love and see if they need any of the things you might be holding on to. (And if you should ever host a big event in the future, borrow the equipment back from them!)

Most of these solutions require complete honesty and for this you might need to dig deep. Take a fresh look at the object in question, think about how long it has been taking up space and how long it is likely to stay there before you get around to using/needing it – if ever. Part with possessions instead of harbouring guilt every time you glance at them. Imagine the feeling of freedom and clarity that clearing that space could bring – this is a big motivator!

To recap:

Don't let your home become a holding area for belongings you intend to pass to others.

Weigh up the value of items versus the worth you place on the space they take up.

Don't keep too many 'spares' of things that you can usually get hold of more easily as and when you need them.

Consider hiring one-off equipment instead of buying.

Be honest with yourself and visualise the room without the items in it.

In an ideal world

The problem: I 'should' be using it

From juicers to exercise bikes, we have all invested in equipment that we feel we really 'should' use. Often we simply don't have the time in our busy lives to incorporate new fads into our routine. A client I work with turned her spare room into a mini gym, spending hundreds of pounds on equipment only to realise that she enjoyed yoga much more than working out. Accepting that we are not going to use a piece of equipment when we have bought into the idea so enthusiastically can be a real stumbling block. Here are a few helpful points to remember:

Simple steps to a solution

1. Give the item one last chance by putting it in a prominent place. Make it as easy as possible for it to become part of your routine for the next week. If, by the end of that week, the juicer/blender/exercise bike is still untouched, then it is time to move it on. If you aren't making use of something during its last-chance period, donate it to a worthwhile cause.

2. Be kind to yourself. Don't beat yourself up about the fact that you haven't used something. We all have busy lives and holding on to something that you really don't have time to use is only going to make you feel worse. Instead, imagine the feeling of moving the item on and visualise the space that will be created. This comes back to being able to feel relaxed in our homes – if we are surrounded by items and equipment that we would like to use but simply don't have time to, this will drag us down and leave us feeling frustrated and as if we have failed. Worrying about the things we *should* be doing and, for whatever reason, can't, can only have a negative impact on our wellbeing. It's time to free ourselves.

3. Could someone else make use of it? I have a client who, like me, suffers from terrible back problems. He can no longer use the golf clubs he bought four years ago. So he made the decision to pass on the equipment, which would otherwise have sat unused and unloved – he has friends with children who can make use of it and who now enjoy great days out having fun and learning a new skill. There's a real buzz to be gained from matching an unused belonging with an appreciative new owner – enjoy it.

4. Be mindful of future spending on health kicks or fads. The simplest solutions are usually the best, and complicated food-preparation equipment which regularly requires taking to pieces and cleaning are simply not practical for those of us with busy lives. Think about it: a bread maker takes up a lot of room on a kitchen worktop – if it's going to be there, it should earn its place. Before you invest in kit for a new sport or hobby, especially if it is bulky, pinpoint time in the next week when you would *actually* use it and bearing this in mind will often mean making a sacrifice in another area.

To recap:

Give the equipment one last chance by putting it in a prominent position to encourage use.

Free yourself from the guilt of hanging on to kit that you won't use.

Pass unused equipment on and enjoy the buzz.

Be wary of investing in gear for new hobbies; borrow or hire it at first if possible.

Letting go can be difficult, but once you have stepped over the emotional obstacles, it is also incredibly liberating. I see people surrounding themselves with unused, unwanted and unloved possessions in the belief that holding on to items connected with loved ones brings them closer to that person and that by catering for all eventualities and 'just in case' scenarios they are actually being 'organised'. For me organisation cannot exist without order, and order means space, calm and clarity. By addressing each of the points listed above I hope you feel empowered to part with the clutter that crowds your space and your mind. Only when you have done this will you be able to enjoy a real sense of order and peace. Basically it boils down to hanging on to what you need and what you love and ditching the rest – the restorative powers of this process are incredible. This isn't just decluttering, it's a life choice.

4

Getting Started

It starts at home . . .

Dear Vicky, we are downsizing and need to get rid of so much stuff! We need you!

Vicky, we have two children and have just found out we are pregnant again! We need a major detox!

Vicky – I'm going back to work after eight years of being an at-home Mum . . . I need to get my life in order!

Vicky – HELP!

While some clients pick up the phone to me at their wits' end with a home that is out of control, plenty just want my help preparing for an event or a new challenge in their life.

I love it when I hear from people who are about to embark on a new chapter, because I know my methods can help them make sure that they are equipped to succeed. There's no doubt that for many a declutter is the last resort – often people reach a low point and realise that something has to change and that's when I get the call. But ideally, if we could all take small steps each day towards instilling a friendly level of organisation into our homes, we could avoid ever being met with that awful overwhelmed feeling. And in the majority of cases I see, the problems stem from clients simply having *too much stuff*.

The monumental changes in life usually come with at least some pre-warning: a house move, new baby, new job. So when you know that you have a major life-change on the horizon, my advice is to take control and make sure that you stay in the driving seat.

We automatically link many life-changing events to raised stress levels and presume as we approach these moments that feeling anxious and out of control will be inevitable, but it doesn't have to be like this! The idea that a particular type of event will definitely lead to stress was scrapped many years ago by the pioneering psychologist Richard Lazarus (1922–2002). According to Lazarus, stress is a two-way process; it involves the production of stressors by the environment, and the response of an individual subjected to these stressors. It's not just the event itself that matters, but how you view that event, how well you have prepared and whether you feel you have the personal resources and support from others to cope. So there we have it – proof, if it was needed, that moving house does not necessarily have to be stressful!

Here are some of the common situations in which I help clients prepare for change and points to consider for each new challenge, just to illustrate the benefits of taking control at home. Whatever journey we face, the first steps always start at home.

A new healthy start

Starting a new diet or exercise regime? It's a common scenario: you've signed up to the gym and you've invested in a juicer and the exercise gear ... but however good your intentions are, if you haven't prepared your home I believe you are much less likely to keep it up. Before you commit to an exercise programme, help set yourself up for success by decluttering and reorganising your space so that it works with this new beginning.

Dedicate a drawer or basket just for sportswear and keep it within easy reach. Have whatever you need organised and ready to go. We've all been in the situation where the smallest factor influences our split-second decision whether to go for a run or not. If there's *any* excuse, we will take it – so don't let the fact that you don't know where your kit is be the reason you don't push yourself out of the door.

If you are joining the juicing craze, or embarking upon any other eating regime that requires kitchen equipment, then make sure that your juicer/smoothie maker/spiraliser is in a prominent position in your kitchen. It's common sense really, but you're much more likely to stick to a regime if you have organised the relevant area of your home to make it easy for yourself.

A new baby

Whether this is your first, second or third child (or fourth, or fifth!), feeling organised will help you manage the challenges that babies present. Once the new arrival is here, there will be little time for clearing out and sorting so it's important to get easy and reliable systems in place while you can, to help you stay in control.

Babies grow out of outfits so fast, so try keeping boxes neatly labelled '0–6 months' and so on, meaning that as soon as clothes become too small you have an easy, organised space for them instead of piling them in different corners.

Set up 'changing stations' around the house with wipes, nappies and nappy sacks, and fold-up mats close to hand. Make life easier . . . think ahead!

Declutter and clear an accessible cupboard so that you have a place ready for bottles, breast pumps and, when the time comes, weaning snacks and equipment. It's amazing how much stuff such a small person can need – this isn't something you want to be dealing with when sleep-deprived and rushed off your feet.

If you are bottle-feeding, imagine how much more streamlined the sterilisation process will be if you set up an area in the kitchen with everything you need within reach. And in those moments when you need a quick pick-me-up, you don't want to be rummaging through cupboards for your vital snacks – think how handy it would be to have a dedicated box stocked up and ready.

Allowing yourself preparation time to make small changes in the lead-up to bringing your baby home, and starting motherhood in a place of calm and order, will make a huge difference.

A new job

We know that confidence comes from within and you need to approach a new role feeling in control – and, once again, preparation for this starts at home. Cull and reorganise your wardrobe (see Chapter Five for more detail on this) and create a new section for your work outfits. How will your new job impact on your home life? You'll still have the same household tasks but perhaps less time to do them. Putting systems in place so that your home is organised will help you feel more at ease in your new job. Perhaps you will arrive home later in the evening, in which case the time you have to yourself will become even more precious – so make sure that your home is calm, streamlined and ordered, allowing you to feel relaxed when you walk through the front door, helping maintain a work/life balance and not adding to your anxiety!

A new house

Picture yourself in your new home with the right boxes in the right rooms, calmly unpacking your carefully stored, treasured belongings, ready to create a new chapter for them and for you. This *is* achievable. Thorough preparation for a house move can really limit the stress experienced, leaving you to focus on the excitement and the adventure of shaping a new home. Packing in the right way will mean you don't unpack in the wrong way. Packing up all your belongings provides a great opportunity to simplify the way you live by parting with some of them instead of paying to store or move unwanted stuff. See Chapter Ten for more advice on moving.

A new school

The school rush doesn't have to be a mad dash out of the door, toast in hand, uniform still damp from the tumble dryer. Imagine you and your little/big ones waking from a night's sleep in calm, organised bedrooms, picture the ease of pulling uniform items from a neat drawer full of only those that fit, taking the PE kit from its ordered, dedicated space and selecting a few items from a basket full of lunchbox-ready snacks before picking up school shoes which are exactly where they should be ... Sounds good, doesn't it? Having a place for everything really does make life run more smoothly.

And it doesn't have to be only the monumental changes that can benefit from a declutter – smaller events like hosting a party, even if it's only a casual gathering, can be simple and stress-free if you have achieved a level of organisation at home. Socialising should be fun for the host too – make it easy for yourself by having glassware, cutlery and crockery organised so that you are not rushing around trying to lay your hands on the right glasses either before or during your soirée.

Bite-sized chunks

Hands up those who don't have enough hours in the day! Well, my hand is well and truly up and I'm guessing yours is too. I juggle running my businesses, a social life, seeing family, the odd bit of exercise (my hula hoop!) and of course some time for my wellbeing – and most days I feel every minute is accounted for. The majority of people don't have whole days free that they can allocate to reorganising their wardrobe or decluttering their kitchen – and they are usually setting themselves up for failure if they try. Clearly I *do* spend days at a time on such tasks (it's my job!) but I would not necessarily encourage everyone to tackle their own home in this way, especially those with busy lives. The key to a successful declutter is breaking the job down into small, bite-sized chunks.

DON'T BITE OFF MORE THAN YOU CAN CHEW

Occasionally I help clients who have approached a huge task believing they will get through it in a day and then, for various everyday-life reasons, end up abandoning the whole project. Often what's left, through having to stop mid-task, is worse than what they started with. Trust my experience here: tackling an area properly (and I mean to do the job really, really well, to a level that makes total sense) will take longer than you think. It just isn't practical to view a room, or even all of your clothes, as a task that you can get through all in one go. Yes, it could be done, but not to a standard that will have long-term benefits for you – and here's why . . .

You are likely to run out of time

Very often I arrive at a client's house to find the entire contents of their wardrobe spread all over a room. They pulled everything out, thinking they could complete the job in no time at all ... and only a few hours in realised that it was going to take *far* longer than they imagined.

You will get bored

Methodically sorting through drawers and shelves, one after the other, takes more concentration than you might think. My clients are exhausted by the end of the day – not because I've had them running around, but because the amount of mental energy that the declutter demands far outweighs the physical side of things. A couple of hours in and you'll probably find that the novelty of how wonderfully efficient you are being will have worn off and you'll be daunted by the realisation of how long the job is going to take. My guess is you'll be sneaking off to take refuge in the contents of the fridge, TV or social media.

You will run out of steam and stop working efficiently

Focusing on which items to keep and which to move on takes mental and emotional energy; you need to be ruthless with yourself as you make decisions. Sustaining that level of objectiveness over a length of time is tiring and you will find yourself taking the easy option, bundling belongings back into a drawer, convincing yourself you do need/want them because it will be easier than making an honest decision. I usually deter clients from booking me for any more than two days in a row – the mental strain becomes too much. Working fast and furiously under such pressure can mean you later question decisions you've made.

You will feel overwhelmed

Before you empty all of your kitchen cupboards and drawers out at once, think how stressful the sight of that clutter all over your worktops will be. Where will you start? Anxiety levels will rise and something which, if broken down into achievable chunks, could be cathartic and empowering will seem a daunting, impossible task.

Now imagine how satisfying it would be to set yourself a smaller challenge – say, reorganising one drawer, going through its contents carefully and thoroughly and completing the task without rushing. Trust me, the buzz you will get from this will give you more satisfaction than you think. Closing that drawer, knowing its contents are in order, all clutter removed, will be the biggest motivator that you need. I know you'll be fuelled to tackle another drawer, maybe not straight away, but at the next opportunity. Aim to set aside a small period of time every day to keep the flow going, but don't put yourself under pressure if you miss a day – just pick it up as soon you can. Let your decluttering motto be 'little and often'.

Too often these days we are all about the quick fix; we crave instant results and gratification. But if we want to properly overhaul the way our homes are organised we have to break the task down – it is unlikely that your entire home can be decluttered in one big hit. Our busy lifestyles just don't allow it ... unless of course I come knocking at your door! Instead of setting our sights on the end goal, we need to delight in the small steps that we can take on the way. And, believe me, dramatic results can be achieved over just a couple of weeks.

Think of this as 'mindful decluttering' and follow these simple rules in areas you might be tackling at home or work:

Choose a small cupboard, drawer or area.

Make sure you have your bags for rubbish and charity ready.

Dedicate twenty minutes to sorting the contents of the place you've chosen, without interruptions if possible. Allow yourself to become totally immersed in the task.

Methodically go through the contents, reassessing what stays and what goes, focusing on one item at a time.

Don't become distracted or worry about areas of the room yet to be tackled.

Put any 'sentimental' items to one side to look at properly later, not now.

Clean the area, for a fresh start.

Neatly replace the relevant items back in the drawer in categories.

Enjoy the satisfaction you get when the task is completed and feel that just-tidied buzz.

Imagine this level of organisation applied to every area of your home.

Believe me, if you scare yourself by biting off more than you can chew, you risk abandoning the task and putting it off for weeks, months or even years. This method eases you in and once you get started, you'll just want to keep going.

This is a process that doesn't have to start and finish abruptly – once you have embarked on a declutter you will, maybe weeks or months later, revisit areas that you have already tackled and feel able to move on. More items, things you initially wanted to hold on to may later seem out of place in your newly organised space. The initial declutter will be the catalyst for a new approach and you will become braver and bolder in your desire to live with less. One client made a great comparison when she likened the stages of a declutter to plucking up the courage to have a daring haircut.

For me it was like having my hair cut into a short bob – I knew I wanted to do it but didn't feel brave enough, so I had it cut to shoulder length and that gave me the courage to have it bobbed. Step by step, that's clearly how I work.

Jacki, 58

I cannot stress enough how motivational the feeling of completing a task like this will be – even when applied to the smallest areas. The process is infectious and you will be itching to get on to the next challenge. Before you know it you will become an organisational geek (like me!) and you'll find yourself showing off your ordered cupboards to friends and family, passing on the buzz.

Blocking

I have organised my home so that it works *with* me and *for* me. My shelves, cupboards and surfaces are streamlined and clutter-free. Any obstacles that will prevent me moving freely or easily accessing the things I need have been moved. Part of this process has been identifying items which I refer to as 'blocks':

objects that are positioned without care, which make reaching or seeing other possessions more difficult or irritating. I see 'blocking' in most homes, and the busier we are, the more we put things down or away around the house without thought, making life harder for ourselves.

To explain what I mean, here are a few classic 'blocks':

Ornaments and photos on shelves in front of a row of books. You are much less likely to ever read those books if there are knick-knacks in the way.

A coffee-table book which has a few bits and bobs on top. It is unlikely anyone will pick that lovely book up to have a flick through if there are things on top of it.

Jars in front of a row of cereal boxes. In the busy morning rush, moving the jars will be enough of a hassle to put us off reaching for them.

Toys on the lid of a toy chest. This means children are unlikely to play with the contents of the chest, they'll just concentrate on the ones on the top.

Gadgets in your cupboard hidden by other items in front. Bits of kit are far less likely to be used if you have placed other items in front of them that will need moving out of the way first.

Anything standing between you and the object you are trying to reach is something that I would class as a block. I believe that, with the busy lives we lead, having the contents of our home totally accessible is key to streamlined, stress-free living. We need to ensure there is nothing physically between us and the things that we regularly need. Life can feel like one big rush and moving items out of the way to be able to reach other belongings is not an efficient use of time. It might seem like a little thing – how hard is it, after all, to move a jam jar off the shelf to reach a box of cornflakes? But under pressure the slightest extra hurdle seems like a big deal – the decision to bother with breakfast can be made in a nanosecond.

Look around your own home and think of things you frequently find yourself moving or pushing to the side in order to get to something else. Or think of the things you want to use more but know that you don't because getting to them is a pain – just the thought of it is a hassle. Unless grabbing something is quick and easy, often we do without.

It's a symptom of the way we live that we expect everything to be instant; we leave the house in a rush and snatch and grab items quickly on our way out of the door. The key is to think twice when you tidy away your belongings – mis-positioning items can have a knock-on effect. Throughout the chapters that follow, you will implement systems in your home that will involve prioritising everything in order of how accessible you need each item to be.

Temporary states of disorder

Life doesn't always run smoothly – in fact, for many of us it rarely does! By implementing a friendly level of organisation at home we should be able to weather any rough patches, big or small, knowing that order is never far away and we can easily get our space back on track. Once you have decluttered your home and organised your belongings, then there's no need to let a bit of disorder send you into a panic. Our houses are not show homes, they are places to live, laugh and love in, and I want you to feel proud of your space, but not obsessive about keeping it 'just so'.

Even the tidiest of us have messy moments – from

throwing our tops all over the bedroom as we decide what to wear on a night out, to using every pot and pan as we pull out all the stops and cook a fancy meal . . . that's just part of life. An organised home has systems in place, and when chaos strikes it doesn't take too long to restore order because everything has a place and can be tidied away easily and efficiently.

TOO MESSY   JUST RIGHT   OVER THE TOP!

What I'm saying is, don't get hung up on ideas of perfection – it's a state not worth aspiring to, and even if it were achievable for a brief moment, it would never last! Setting ourselves unrealistic goals can mean that we are constantly disappointed when we do not achieve them – studies have shown that perfectionism can cause anxiety and depression (Flett, Hewitt and Heisel, *Review of General Psychology*, 2014.) So don't become the host who clears away the crumbs that fall as your guest bites into a piece of cake. Don't become obsessed with every little detail around the house – mess can be tidied later. Let the children go crazy with their toys – being untidy and messy can be part of their natural creative process and order can always be restored later.

There's no need to panic if my home gets turned upside down by the kids. I now feel that everything has a place and nothing takes too long to tidy. Once Vicky explained that getting organised wouldn't mean having to keep everything looking absolutely perfect, I could feel my anxiety levels drop! The kids now know where everything belongs and even help to tidy up!

Sue, 45

Once you have followed my methods and streamlined your home, there should be no worry that – after all your wonderful efforts – you will lose control again. I truly believe that once you have sampled Simple Living, you will naturally enjoy living with less and keeping what you have organised in a way that works for you. Sometimes it doesn't happen all in one go – even when you think you have worked through every room and applied all of my methods, there may still be tweaks to make in areas where you could be more thorough. It can be that temporary states of disorder highlight those areas – when tidying away is not as straightforward as it could be, or when you realise that your storage isn't working as efficiently as it might. This is the time to make those adjustments – you will make the final touches to your home as you go about living your life: that is, when the systems we put in place get put to the ultimate test.

Start with your sock drawer . . . and the rest will follow

So, here we are. Consider this the start of your decluttering journey; the day you turned the tide on chaos in your home and took back control! I'm going to show you how to get the decluttering buzz from something as simple as a sock drawer – when I talked about bite-sized chunks, I wasn't joking. I've tried and tested this simple start-off challenge with so many people and it spurred all of them on to do more. From a messy teen to a stay-at-home mum – I guarantee that doing this will make a difference!

If you have time to read this book right now, then you have a moment to carry out this simple task before you move on to the next chapter. Completing it will set you up for all that follows. Remember, instilling organisation in our homes is not a giant task, it's a series of smaller chores that we can *all* make time for, however hectic our lives may be. Let's get started. Humour me and just try this . . .

Empty the contents of your sock drawer onto a clear surface or the floor. Wipe the drawer out for a fresh beginning.

Discard any worn-out, odd, uncomfortable socks or those that you just don't like.

Match all the socks into pairs and put into balls for a tidy look.

Put them back into the drawer in basic categories: daily; sports; bed; posh etc., with the most often worn category at the front of the drawer, least worn at the back.

Bag up the discarded socks and get rid!

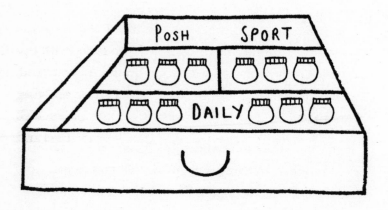

OK, I know it's not rocket science. But in the morning, when you go to choose your socks, I guarantee you'll get a real buzz from the level of order in that drawer. No more rooting around among never worn socks, delving through odd or holey socks – instead, uncluttered organisation. You will enjoy the satisfaction from completing this simple task and feel inspired to apply the resulting sense of harmony to all areas in your precious space. This should set you on a journey on which you declutter and organise, bit by bit.

As you'll have gathered, the exercise is not just about socks. I'm showing you how what might seem like a giant, overwhelming task – decluttering and organising your home – can be broken down into a series of straightforward jobs. By keeping things simple you can maintain the same level of enthusiasm and energy from start to finish.

It's that basic – start with your sock drawer and see what happens. Don't do anything further that day. Just start, sort and complete successfully.

Throughout the chapters that follow I will show you how to break rooms and areas down into tasks, with tips and advice for every part of your home. As you read, I know that you will be inspired to declutter, to bring order and to find your own form of Simple Living. Fall back in love with your home again and let calmness and serenity be yours!

5

Clothes

Getting your wardrobe sorted

I had so many clothes, I had to pile them up in the corner of the room because my wardrobe was overflowing – but somehow every morning I felt like I had nothing to wear. Vicky has totally transformed the way I organise and display my clothes. She's made me reassess what is worth keeping and what I should get rid of. It's such a great start to the day to open the wardrobe and choose from a neat selection of clothes, all of which I know I like and that fit me. Getting dressed and choosing an outfit has become enjoyable again.

Karen, 33

Does this sound familiar? Believe me, you are not alone in wondering why, when you have so many items to choose from, you still feel you have nothing to wear. And as a result of feeling like this you probably buy more clothes, adding to the clutter, and the vicious circle continues. Deep down most of us can recognise when a situation is out of control, but mustering the time and energy that we think we will need to address it puts us off doing anything at all. Reorganising a wardrobe *is* a mammoth task. Whatever you do, do not be tempted to set off thinking you can plough through it in a few hours. Once you've pulled everything out, you will be amazed, possibly a little embarrassed and *definitely* overwhelmed by how much you have and how long it will take to sort through. Wardrobes are like the TARDIS – my clients are always shocked at how much comes out. Seeing your clothes in a different layout – i.e. in piles on the bed – makes you realise just how many you have. Clothes are fun and getting dressed every morning should be a pleasure, but when opening our wardrobe presents us with rails of chaos, too much choice and an array of clothes that we don't even like or that don't fit, enjoyment is replaced by anxiety.

In order to clear our minds we must first clear the space that we view every day. In the same way that we organise paperwork, we can 'file' our clothes to make the daily decision about what to wear so much easier. We can filter out the old, unworn, ill-fitting and unwanted, leaving only those pieces that make us feel confident to step out and face the day.

I predict that once you have completed every area of your wardrobe you will keep going back and realising that it is time to let go of more and more clothes. You will feel less fear about letting go. Only then will you start valuing each item of clothing, respecting everything that remains in your wardrobe and changing your spending habits when it comes to buying more clothes. A great benefit of a wardrobe sort-out is that you are likely to come across clothes that you haven't worn for ages, simply because they were lost behind piles of newer purchases and you'd forgotten you had them. It's a wonderful feeling when old favourites are rediscovered.

There are no set rules for deciding what to let go of and what to keep. How could I set anything in stone when everyone's situation is so different? However, by following the tasks below you will find yourself able to make these decisions yourself and do so with confidence. The purpose is to empower you to take control of your wardrobe and to put a level of organisation in place that you will want to maintain – over time this will become a habit rather than an effort.

The sciencey bit!

Having a wardrobe that works for you really does make a difference to your daily life, because having easy access to clothes that you like and that suit you affects your mood – it's official!

According to social psychologist Gauri Sarda-Joshi, the clothes we wear affect our behaviour, attitudes, personality, mood, confidence – and even the way we interact with others. This is called 'enclothed cognition'. Sarda-Joshi believes that we also judge ourselves and our roles based on what we are wearing, because of the way clothes can make us feel. This means that wearing certain outfits can subtly affect our attitude and behaviour, so let's make sure that our wardrobes contain only those outfits that make us shine.

If you have sorted out your sock drawer then you should already be feeling the benefits, as Sarda-Joshi says that even our *underwear* affects the way we feel about ourselves! She believes that hidden clothes like our socks and underwear have a strong influence on the way we see ourselves and on our confidence levels.

Tackling your wardrobe will enhance your life in many ways, so I'll break this down into small and manageable tasks.

Task 1: Creating space

Let's start by clearing some space in your daily wardrobe. This is the most accessible part of your wardrobe – the rails, shelves and drawers. There is no point in an item living here that you would only wear a few times a year, you can create space for it elsewhere in your home – possibly in a spare-room wardrobe or under the bed. As long as this is done neatly, don't worry too much whether it's folding or hanging space you have available.

Occasional wear

Unless you are a nipping out to black-tie dos on a regular basis, there is no need to have formal and evening wear taking up valuable space in your daily wardrobe space. If you have a spare room with a wardrobe, then use it to store your posh frocks. But before you move them, be sure to reassess whether or not they are still loved, the right size and ever likely to be worn again. Any item that doesn't pass these tests will be wasting precious storage space. Are the days of the sequinned black mini-dress from your twenties numbered? If so, say goodbye!

Wedding and bridesmaid's dresses are generally bulky and can use up valuable space in our daily storage. When friends or family have forked out for expensive bridesmaid's dresses clients often feel obliged to hang on to them, wary of their cost. I have a few suggestions ...

Have a conversation with the bride letting her know your intentions, and check if she has a preference as to where the dress should go or which charity could benefit from its sale.

Your bridesmaid's dress could be someone else's prom dress – think about how it could be given a new life. There are many charity shops that take wedding dresses, some even specialise in bridal wear.

Search online for 'wedding dress charities' and you will not believe the uses that can be found for your dress, you will find many inspiring stories.

If you do decide to store your dress it is essential to get it professionally cleaned first, or any marks or stains will worsen over time. Many dry-cleaners offer the service of wrapping the dress safely for storage, which is a good option.

Ensure you store the remaining special garments safely. I love clear shoulder covers which protect the top of dresses and jackets from dust. I also put anti-moth sachets and cedar spray regularly anywhere I am storing clothes. Always check the environment is not damp – the little critters love it! Make sure nothing is stored in sunlight, and if an item is heavy or has gems or sequins then folding and wrapping it in acid-free tissue is best, as hanging heavy items long-term can pull or stretch the fabric.

Seasonal storage

Removing clothes that cannot be worn in the current season can double the amount of space in your wardrobe. Neatly fold away any items which are out of season and place in labelled clear plastic boxes – remember to include footwear; there is no point having chunky winter boots taking up valuable storage in your daily wardrobe space when months will go by without you wearing them. As you pack these clothes away, be sure to put aside for charity any items that are not worth keeping because of their size, condition or style.

Storing away items like this is a great way of having a natural cull both when you pack them and when, later in the year, you unpack them. You will find yourself reluctant to put back into your neat and streamlined wardrobe any clothes which you don't genuinely love or know you won't wear.

Remember, this is a job that needs doing only twice a year, in the lead-up to the summer or winter months. The less you own, the easier it is, and it's the perfect way to remind yourself what you actually have.

Holiday box

We all have items that we wouldn't be brave enough or warm enough in to wear at home but which we love to throw on during our holidays. For clients who enjoy regular breaks in the sun, I often suggest a holiday box. If you're one of those sun-worshippers pop all your sundresses and exotic beachwear into a neatly labelled box, or perhaps a spare-room drawer, and enjoy the ease of holiday packing when it is time to jet off somewhere sunny! I'm sure you'll find that, as before, when you store away and then rediscover items like this, a natural culling process occurs – you will spot those clothes that no longer fit your style or size and use this as a reason to move them on.

Task 2: Section by section

Imagine opening the wardrobe doors to rails of ordered clothes, shelves of neatly folded tops, drawers with streamlined, organised contents: being presented only with outfits that you love, that fit you and that you feel confident to wear.

This can be achieved successfully if you tackle the wardrobe correctly and break the job down by following these simple steps. As with everything, I would not advise you to empty your entire wardrobe out at once because you will underestimate how long it will take to sort through and replace the clothing you're keeping without getting completely and utterly overwhelmed, bored or very tired!

So, follow my advice and work bit by bit. Choose a specific drawer, rail or shelf and go through the following process. Don't overstretch yourself by biting off more than you can chew – choose an area and work through these simple steps; you'll be so pleased with what you achieve that you'll be itching to tackle another section.

Choose which area you are going to sort – i.e. a section of rail, a drawer or a shelf.

Have some charity and rubbish bags ready.

Make sure your bed is made neatly as you will use this as a sorting area.

Pull out everything from your chosen section on to the bed and put it into piles. No need to categorise at this point, let's keep it simple.

If you come across clothes that need repairing or altering, put these in a separate pile.

Now, go through each pile in turn, piece by piece, and ask yourself the following questions before choosing whether to bin, pass on, bag up for charity or keep.

Do you like it on you?

Not on the hanger in the shop, or on the model online – I mean do you like it on *yourself*? There is a big difference. I'm always drawn to long floaty hippy-style tops – I love them, but I've learnt that they don't flatter me and never look as I've imagined they will . . . so now I steer clear of these when shopping. In reassessing previous purchases like this you will learn to become a more mindful shopper in the future. You don't want to end up with a rail of clothes that stay hanging in your wardrobe (looking lovely and floaty!) but will never see the light of day.

Are you keeping it 'just in case'?

We all have items that fit and suit us but the right occasion to wear them just never seems to come around. We hang on to them, for years, just in case that niche situation arises. When I see rails of party dresses taking up space in bedrooms or bulging out of spare-room wardrobes in a client's home, I know that it's time for me to have words! Be honest with yourself. What is more valuable right now: the space, or the dress you may never wear again? Are you going to say goodbye now or store it for five years unworn and *then* do it?

Does it fit properly?

Everything you wear should make you feel good – from your work outfits to your pyjamas. Details like the cut of a top's neckline or the length of its sleeves can put us off wearing it, because we know our shape and what makes us feel confident and, perhaps more importantly, what doesn't. If we find a shirt too clingy or too short (this is my personal issue!) then, however lovely it may be, we know in our heart of hearts that we will not wear it because these details will niggle at us all day and often make us feel self-conscious. Pass these items on and make someone else happy.

Is it the right size?

Or is it the size that you would *like* to be? And here I might need to be a little brutal. Keeping clothes that you know you will wear when you lose a few pounds is fine if you are actively striving towards a weight-loss goal. However, if you are hanging on to a large amount of clothes that are a couple of sizes too small and they are taking up space in your daily wardrobe, this isn't positive. You shouldn't have to fight with your wardrobe when you get dressed in the morning.

Some of my clients like to have one item that is too small hanging up so they see it. They say it gives them inspiration. That's fine. But any more than this can have the opposite effect. Don't torture yourself and pull your mood down every day. Live in the now, as well as looking forward to the future.

I ask clients to go through each 'future' item and put key pieces into a small storage box. I'm talking a selected few. Because realistically when they get back to their goal weight, they will want to buy new, more current pieces. The well-deserved purchases! I'm not encouraging you to be wasteful, just realistic. Picture how much better you would feel if you opened your wardrobe to see a rail of clothes that all fitted you comfortably and made you feel happy about the shape you are. That's the way it should be.

Is it beyond repair?

Have you worn it to death and got all of the wear out of it you possibly could? Items we love can end up beyond repair and at that point it's time to let go. It might be your favourite old woolly sweater, but if you haven't worn it for months because it is threadbare on the elbows and you also haven't got around to sorting a repair job then it's now or never. While we should treasure clothes (and all other belongings), there is also a point at which we need to recognise that certain items might be past their best and the effort and money involved to get them back to where we want them may be pointless.

If you have a few items falling into this category, make a 'repair and alterations' pile to assess at the end of the task. This should go straight to the front door to take to be repaired or dealt with yourself immediately. Most clients look at this pile at the end of the task and admit they don't wish to spend the money or time to make this happen. Again, it's not about being wasteful, just a matter of being realistic about what is worth hanging on to.

Would someone else enjoy this more than you?

The formal coat that you don't feel comfortable in or the skater-style dress that you feel too old to wear should not be cluttering up your wardrobe. Move them on to someone who will treasure and enjoy them – and if you have no one in mind send them to a charity shop. When choosing items to pass on, don't get bogged down with the worry of how much you spent on them or hung up on the fact they might still have their tags on. (We've all done it!) For today you will feel guilty, but embrace it and accept it, because tomorrow, when you experience the joy of a streamlined selection of clothes, you will naturally move on.

Remember the student I mentioned earlier, hunting for charity shop bargains? Well it's not just Granny's coat she may love – she could well be looking for something cool to wear for a night out. Imagine her joy at coming across your favourite dress – the one that has been sitting at the back of your wardrobe in the dark for the last ten years – and falling in love with it. Instantly it is given another ten years of wear – a whole new life!

I love that thought. Look at the pieces lurking at the back or your wardrobe: are you going to leave them to fester there or let someone else enjoy them? It's ten years of dark vs ten years of love! The trend for second-hand/pre-loved clothing is still going strong. Sign up for Gift Aid at your local charity shop and when you receive that wonderful email telling you how much money your donations have made, give a little cheer!

What's next?

You should now have a smaller selection of clothes ready to put back into your wardrobe. At this stage, I always encourage my clients to go easy on themselves if they haven't got rid of as much as they had hoped or expected to. Sometimes it can be harder than we initially think, and I call the process you have just been through Stage One. Stage Two happens in the following days. It's the moment when you look at your beautiful freshly organised wardrobe, and the items you knew, deep down, you shouldn't be keeping, the ones you hesitated over, suddenly look out of place. These items will stand out because they don't belong, they are ruining the good job you've done. I predict that you will take them out and allow yourself a moment to feel smug, knowing you've cracked it!

When Vicky helped me go through my totally out-of-control wardrobe I was so happy with the results and it was lovely not to have so much to wade through. The next day I felt like I'd been shopping! Over the few weeks after Vicky left I gradually got rid of more and more, exactly as she predicted I would.

Ceri, 36

Everyone's approach to how they store and display their clothes is different – the main point is to display them so that you can see easily, at a glance, exactly what you have. There is no one system to suit all, as we all have different quantities of clothing and varying amounts of storage.

Now, for tips on how to replace, store and display your clothes read the relevant section below, depending on which section you're tackling.

Getting it right: hanging rails

I couldn't even see most of my clothes. I had tried to squeeze so much in that everything on the rail was bunched up, with hangers all catching on each other and getting tangled every time I tried to pull something out. I started to avoid opening the wardrobe at all and dressed from a pile of old faithful items – I knew then that I needed to do something!

Lindsey, 41

Is your hanging rail bowing under the strain of a mismatch of overloaded hangers? Or are you wasting space with bulky wooden ones? When it comes to deciding how to organise your clothes on the rail, I can't stress enough how important having the right hangers is to the way you will view your wardrobe. A messy selection of mismatched hangers will never look or feel ordered, and using metal hangers on jumpers and knitwear can leave tell-tale bumps or ridges on the shoulders. In my experience investing in good hangers is as important as investing in the right clothes.

I recommend skinny hangers (see the recommended suppliers list on page 195 – and be aware that you can order in different sizes!) which take up half the room of wooden hangers and so save valuable space. The more room you have spare, the easier it is to flick through your clothes and see, at a glance, what you have. As with everything in your home, you are more likely to use it if it is easy to see and to access.

I love this wardrobe I designed for a client who was lucky enough to be able to build what they needed from scratch. It had the perfect amount of space for the clothes they actually had – not what they thought they had! The basic principles of this design can be adapted to suit any room.

When you start hanging clothes back on the rail, decide how you are going to categorise them. This is a personal decision and there is no one-rule-fits-all approach. Many of my clients like to arrange their clothes in order of colour, which provides a great overall visual effect when you open the wardrobe doors in the morning. If you have specific work clothes, then you might like to create a section on the rail for these. Or you might like to organise into very basic item categories: trousers, skirts, shirts and so on. The key thing is that your 'daily clothes' are the most accessible. For me daily clothes are casual, so I always keep the jeans next to the T-shirts and tops that I wear to work – all within easy reach.

However you choose to place them on the rail, I know that if you arrange them neatly, on matching hangers, you are much more likely to put them back nicely and to get more wear out of your selection.

Storage tip: The aim is to avoid any dead space within the storage in your bedroom. If possible, consider moving the rail in your wardrobe up higher. This will not only prevent clothes dragging on the floor or the base of the wardrobe unit, but it will also open up space, especially under shorter hanging items, to store shoes or bags and other smaller things.

Getting it right: folding

Shelves

If you are an organisational geek like me, you will get a real kick out of the piles of neatly folded clothes on display in shops. But you can also have that level of order in your own wardrobe by following my simple advice – and once your shelves of clothes are looking lovely and neat you will want to keep them that way, trust me.

How to Fold:

1. SINGLE FOLD

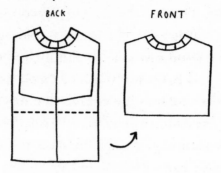

BACK   FRONT

2. TRIPLE FOLD

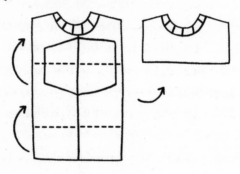

3. QUARTER FOLD

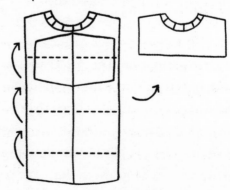

Shelves that are at eye level and below are for the clothes that you need to see and access most often. Fold them as they often appear in shops – I call this a single fold. These items can be placed one on top of the other – if it helps you to use a folding board this could be a good investment, although after a while it will become a habit and you'll probably find you don't need one. By folding the clothes and displaying them this way, everything will be easily visible. This is the key: having clear storage makes the daily decision what to wear just as clear.

When you need to take an item from one of these lovely neat piles, make sure that you bring down the *whole pile* rather than grabbing from the middle and upsetting the lot. Put it on a flat surface and take what you need before replacing the whole pile on the shelf. This technique is easy to get used to and ensures that you don't disrupt your streamlined piles every time you remove a piece of clothing.

Categorise clothes in a way that suits you. Again, there's no point in me issuing rules for storage that are too precise – everyone has a different selection of clothes and varying amounts of storage available to them. You will know what makes sense for you. I love having all of my 'comfy' clothes together, knowing that I can head straight for that shelf when I get home from work, desperate to get out of what I've been wearing all day. A lot of it is common sense and there's no need for me to complicate it by making rules for the sake of it!

Drawers

Drawers require a different approach: there is no point creating a neat pile of clothes then placing the whole pile in a drawer, because you'll only see what's on top, and trying to look for anything at the bottom will involve pulling out the whole lot. Here it makes sense to store clothes vertically, quarter- or triple-folded and lined up one behind the other. When you pull the drawer out, you will see clearly everything that it contains.

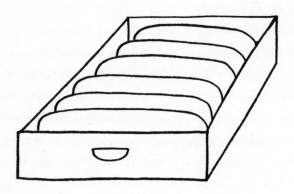

Task 3: Underwear

As with all drawers – the first step is to empty the contents on to a clear surface and to have a cull! Once you have the contents laid out in front of you, the unworn and the worn-out items will stand out. Then when you have binned the unwanted you will find, with fewer items, that everything is so much easier to store and my guess is you won't miss what has gone.

Here are my top tips for undies!

Pants

There are those who choose to immaculately fold their pants and those who don't. I'm firmly in the don't camp – life's too short! But whether you fold or not, it is worth investing in some drawer dividers, which are readily available these days and cheap to buy. (Again, see my recommended suppliers list on page 195.) Simply place these in your drawers and separate the pants by category or colour.

If you are a 'folder', then pants should be stored vertically/side by side, not one on top of the other, so that you can see what you have. As far as thongs go, I can't imagine anyone folding them, but each to their own!

I have my occasional items in a separate drawer – things like shape wear, control wear and strapless bras – these, as always, follow the 'occasional wear' rule, meaning they don't need to take up storage in your daily space.

Bras

Store bras one behind the other, vertically. I like to fold my bras in half, tucking the straps behind and, if in sets with matching knickers, I always also tuck them behind the corresponding bra.

When buying bra sets it's a good idea to always buy two pairs of knickers to every bra. Knickers tend to get washed a lot more and will therefore fade faster. Bearing this in mind, from now onwards put your bras from sets in the wash more often that you usually would.

Socks

If you're following my advice to the letter, then this drawer will already have been sorted! But if not, quite simply tuck those tails in and ball them – this is the only effort a pair of socks needs (see page 67).

Tights

Shake tights out and flatten them before folding them repeatedly until they fit in your hand. You can then store them vertically in your drawer. Most clients are surprised when they see their tights lined up side by side at how many pairs they actually own!

Task 4: Shoes and other accessories

So many of my clients have admitted that they forgot about shoes when planning bedroom storage, or underestimated how much space they need. Simply allowing room underneath a hanging rail or at the base of a shelving unit is often not enough.

But there are also those who have gone in for quirky shoe-storage solutions. Don't do it! The best approach, as ever, is to keep it simple. No baskets, wire trays or shelves at angles. All you need is a clear shelf. If you are lucky enough to be getting a new wardrobe, then plan in some adjustable shelves to allow for shoes and boots – which obviously vary so much in height. You don't want a large gap of dead space above your flats and pumps – ideally you need to be able to lower the shelf above and adjust the shelving to fit changing needs and seasons. Also, make sure that the shelves are wide and deep enough – it's no use having a shelf the width or depth of three shoes. Don't forget to store seasonal shoes away when they are not in use.

I recently advised a client who had no shoe storage in her wardrobes to buy a set of wide adjustable book-shelves. She also bought an extra shelf (that lived flat at the bottom, unseen when not in use) to insert in the summer months to allow for storage of more flat shoes. For a better visual, have shoes with the toes facing towards you. If you don't have the money/space for purpose-built shoe storage then the bookshelf solution is perfect.

Bags

After ensuring that all your bags are loved, wanted and needed in your life, store them away safely – ideally upright on a shelf. Pack them with tissue to ensure they keep their shape. Covering them in a dust bag will mean they stay protected, but will hide them from your view; and bearing in mind that if you can't see some-thing you'll usually forget it's there, you need to weigh up your personal options here, perhaps depending on the value of the bags. If you are one of those well co-ordinated fashionistas who change their bags to suit their outfits (I envy your dedication!), then keep them all within easy reach. If, like most of us, you rotate your handbags infrequently, it's fine to pop them higher up or somewhere less accessible.

I recently stopped carrying a daily handbag, mainly because my back isn't great and after years of lugging a heavy weight around on my shoulder I wanted to give my body a rest. After a week of trialling handbag-free living, I realised I didn't miss a thing! My bank cards and cash are stored in my handy phone case wallet and my keys are the only other thing I carry, which fit easily into my coat pocket. It's liberating and I always feel I have less to think about.

Belts

This is totally down to preference, but I personally like to roll belts because I only own a few. I put them in a small basket with other occasionally worn accessories. They certainly don't need a drawer of their own. Many men like to hang their belts on a special hanger, but again a dedicated area of drawer or even a basket underneath the rail that their trousers are hanging on works well too. Rolled belts are easy to find and store neatly.

General tips

Saving special clothes for your children

Some of my friends have items of clothing handed down to them from their mums – special pieces their mothers have treasured. This is a wonderful thing and I sometimes wish my mum had done the same, but as I'm several inches taller than her and a dress size bigger, it wouldn't have worked anyway! When you sort through your clothes you may come across a few special items you can't actually wear but really value and would like to pass on. If so, put them – safely wrapped with moth prevention – in a memory box. (See Chapter Nine for more on how to create your own memory box.)

Under-bed storage

The spaces under beds can be really useful for storage of less-used items but, as always, this must be done neatly. I recommend special under-bed boxes or storage drawers which will help you keep organised. I personally couldn't sleep knowing that I was lying on top of piles of chaos that had been shoved under the bed simply to keep the room looking tidy. Clutter crowds our headspace as much as our physical spaces and just pushing it out of sight doesn't help – deep down we are still aware of its presence and we feel the negativity.

Give yourself a break! Nightwear and sportswear

There are two categories of clothing for which I encourage clients to relax the usual folding rules – we are all busy and really don't need to be worrying about having perfectly folded pyjamas or sports kit. As long as both are stored so that they are easily accessible and visible when you open a door or drawer, then I say let yourself off. A quick rough fold is fine here.

WARNING!

Make sure that the process of organising your clothes and storage does not leave you with a giant 'to do' list. It is easy to put particular piles to one side to deal with later: items to be altered, given to friends, taken to a charity shop or sold. Make it as easy for yourself as possible.

Put bagged clothes for charity straight into your car.

Give friends or family a time limit for them to collect items before they go to charity.

Charities that collect will need to be called in advance so that you can book a time slot. (See page 197 for information.)

Remember some charity shops are happy to take damaged or marked clothes that they cannot sell and send them on for recycling. This can still make them money (a quick phone call is all it takes to check). Many council recycling centres (including those in supermarket car parks) have clothes banks for those items not in good enough condition for charity shops to sell on.

Be kind to yourself and realistic with your time. Items that you no longer want need to leave your house as soon as possible, not loiter in bags by the front door for weeks. This is about you and your new home.

I guarantee that you'll love the space you have created, will embrace having less and will most certainly wonder how you managed to fit so much into your wardrobe in the first place – everyone does. Living with less truly feels like having more when it comes to clothes. You will wear more of what you have, you can enjoy the feeling of getting dressed again and will be more mindful when purchasing new things.

Enjoy the clarity!

6

Toy Storage and Children's Bedrooms

Overwhelmed, drowning in 'stuff' and bombarded with too many choices ... that's not just how *we* feel – I'm talking about how children's lives can easily become just as cluttered as ours. Our children are bombarded with choices every time they glance around their playroom or bedroom: *What to do? What to play with?*

Psychologists tell us that our children are increasingly stressed and anxious, and I believe that chaos in their rooms and playrooms can often be part of the problem. By streamlining bedrooms, playrooms and toy-storage areas we can help children reclaim control of their spaces and allow them to play and grow, free from the anxiety caused by sensory overload.

Kim John Payne, author of *Simplicity Parenting* (2010), recognises the stress brought on by children being overwhelmed with choice. He compares the symptoms that he sees in children in affluent America and Europe, leading apparently 'perfect' lives, to those seen in sufferers of post-traumatic stress. His solution is to limit the choices that our children have to make.

Most of us have seen how children's clutter can quickly take over an entire home – their toys can spill out into every room. Limiting the selection of children's belongings that you choose to keep will make it easier to achieve a simple level of organisation and will encourage respect for possessions.

Although the Montessori approach to education (which focuses on a child's independence, allowing freedom within limits) might not be everyone's choice, I totally agree with Tim Seldin, President of the Montessori Foundation, when he says:

⁶ If children are taught where things belong, and how to return them correctly when they finish using them, they internalize this sense of order, and carry it with them for the rest of their lives ... Most of us can be overwhelmed by the chaos that quickly develops around the house if we leave things lying around. Children are particularly sensitive to this. ⁹

In the same way that opening the door to a messy cupboard raises our stress levels, chaos in children's playrooms or storage areas can leave them feeling just as anxious and overwhelmed. And just as we make a conscious decision not to fight through the clutter to reach the item at the back of the cupboard, they will not see beyond the toys that are most obvious, anything lurking behind will be forgotten. In many of the homes I visit there are simply too many toys and the parents who live there would agree. But, for a variety of different and entirely understandable reasons, a steady tide of possessions continues to flow into their home, adding to the problem.

I know the difference streamlining children's environments can make to how they value and enjoy their possessions, and this is why I love organising children's spaces. By following my simple methods to restore order and calm in your child's space, you can also encourage them to tidy up after themselves. Sounds too good to be true, but it does really happen!

So, we know – and parenting experts back it up – that too many choices and too much clutter are as unhealthy for our children as for us adults. Once again, let's break the task down into manageable pieces and I'll help you to restore order (and sanity!) in little lives. By following the tasks below you can reduce the amount of toys taking over your home, then reorganise them in a way which makes it easy to maintain order.

Too many toys = too many choices!

Most of my friends and the majority of my clients who are parents admit that their children have too much 'stuff' – and they tell me that the more they have, the more they want and the less they value what they already have. It's a vicious circle.

Our parents often hark back to the simplicity of their own childhoods when they had far fewer possessions and seemed to live a less complicated, more carefree existence. We can't turn back time, but we can take positive action to limit the choices today in our children's lives.

> ❝ As parents we ... define ourselves by what we bring our attention and presence to. This is easy to forget when daily life feels more like triage. By eliminating some of the clutter in our lives we can concentrate on what we really value, not just what we're buried under, or deluged with. ❞
>
> Kim John Payne, *Simplicity Parenting*

It's time to help our children enjoy the present moment, to explore what they really value in an atmosphere of calm, not surrounded by an avalanche of belongings.

Often clients tell me that a certain toy is their child's favourite, and I have come to understand the real reason why children get fixated on one possession. They are spoilt with so many other options to play with – shelves full of so many toys but many of them hidden behind each other, as well as piles of games, puzzles and so on. Often the real reason that children seem to ignore the options around them and to focus repeatedly on one toy is that they can't really 'see', with any clarity, what else surrounds them. There is too much disorganisation.

Why do our children have so much?

Before we tackle the chaos, it is worth considering how we got ourselves, and our children, into this state of excess in the first place. Understanding why today's playrooms and bedrooms are bursting with more toys than our parents' generation, or even our own, could ever have dreamt of can help us deal with the issues at the heart of the problem. And although these vary from one home to another, many are rooted in the misconception that more toys = more happiness.

So let's look at how our children's toy boxes came to be bursting, and at my advice on how to shift our perspectives from so much materialism.

Receiving too many toys as Christmas or birthday presents

I have had many mothers tell me that the ridiculous amount of gifts their children end up with after birthday parties makes them feel seriously uncomfortable, but often they think it would seem mean (and would outrage the birthday girl/boy) to put 'no presents please' on the invites.

Try instead: For family members, suggest they club together to buy a gift that will be really valued – something the child needs like a bike, garden play equipment or a special desk. Alternatively, ask that they give an experience – perhaps an outing to the zoo or the cinema, or a ticket for a local attraction. Personally, I don't buy my friends' children birthday presents – I prefer to treat them, when I see them, to something that I know they need or would really value. When planning a large birthday party it's perfectly acceptable to put a note on the invitation along these lines: *Harry already has so many lovely things so please don't feel that you have to bring a gift, but – if you would like to – he really enjoys books*

for bedtime stories, pens and football stickers. At least then you are giving guests a get-out option and providing a constructive list of suggestions for those who would like to buy something. You are taking control!

Using toys as rewards

In clients' and friends' homes I often come across reward charts, jars of marbles and other incentive schemes to try and keep little ones on the straight and narrow. Sometimes the reward is simply a sticker, but on other occasions toys are used as incentives for good behaviour or for completing chores. As with many practices, this doesn't pose a problem if it's a one off, but when children come to expect gifts because they have either completed a chart or done well at school, football or ballet, it adds to the build-up of clutter. And according to many parenting experts, rewards and bribery often produce short-term results and can set up a continuous cycle in which children expect more and more to perform certain tasks or to behave in a certain way.

Try instead: I'm no child-psychology expert, and for me the jury's still out on the pros and cons of rewards for good behaviour, but I do know that praise and encouragement cost nothing, yet are priceless when it comes to children's self-esteem and sense of worth. To paraphrase Gandhi: 'Be the change you want to see in your family.' Leading by example and not bribery will almost certainly have a greater long-term impact than any reward system when it comes to influencing how your children behave. Consider celebrating achievement with a family meal (I don't necessarily mean eating out) – raise a glass to your child's success and see them glow with pride.

Compensating for lack of time

We are all so busy, and working parents have it particularly tough. One minute they're supposed to be baking cupcakes to take for the school's cake sale; the next, carting the children off to a range of extracurricular activities – and often, in between all this, holding down some kind of job! It's no wonder parents often resort to buying a new toy because they feel guilty about not being able to spend 'quality time' with their children. It's easy to lecture parents on how important spending time with their children is, but we can't magic more hours into each day. However, forking out for toys isn't the answer and children won't be fooled – what they want is you!

Try instead: Don't beat yourself up about not being able to allocate whole afternoons or days as quality time with your children, and try instead to focus on making the time that you do have together memorable. This can be in the car on the way to an activity or to school – instead of zoning out listening to the radio while letting the children play on an iPad, use this time to connect with them and let them open up about their day. Make the most of the time that you *do* have, and don't try and distract them from the time you don't have by buying them the latest gizmos and gadgets! Sometimes we simply forget to make the effort to start a conversation.

Buying toys because you went without

Some parents fill their houses with toys for their children to compensate for the fact that they didn't have as much when they were growing up. Funnily enough, it's often the same people who look back on the simplicity of their own childhoods with nostalgia and fondness. The misconception that a happy childhood means one with all the latest toys seems to override fond memories of a simpler, less materialistic happiness.

Try instead: Many of the most successful individuals I've met – the ones with strong work ethics – came from humble backgrounds which have fuelled their determination to succeed. Why then do the same people deny their own offspring the chance to strive for goals by handing them everything they could possibly desire on a plate? Think of your own strengths and feel proud of your achievements – you might still feel bitter about not having the Barbie beach house that your best friend had, but has it really done you any long-term damage?! Chances are it's helped shape you in a positive way. Don't rob your children of the chance to have goals to aim for, or save up for, by drowning them in clutter.

Buying the latest toys because of peer pressure

A report by UNICEF based on a study of 250 children from the UK, Spain and Sweden said 'brand bullying' was most prevalent in the UK, with parents feeling more 'helpless' and unable to resist buying branded goods for their children. The report said that while family time was more of a priority in the other two countries, our society was preoccupied with materialism.

Try instead: Many of the items that children feel they *need* to own to be accepted within a peer group are passing fads: one minute they cannot live without them, the next they are gathering dust in a corner. Try to limit purchases to birthdays and Christmas: ensuring that children have to wait a period of time before receiving something usually tests whether or not they really want it – often they'll have changed their mind. Although saying 'no' is incredibly hard, it's an important life lesson which could help ensure our children are prepared for when they're older and have to manage their own finances and stand strong when others attempt to influence them.

Buying toys to compensate for trauma, illness or disadvantage

When children are poorly or going through a tough time because of family or social issues, parents will of course try anything to put a smile back on their face – that's natural and understandable. This often means a trip down to the toy shop or a flick through a catalogue: *I let him choose something to cheer himself up*, they'll say. However, if the pattern is repeated every time a little one goes through a rough patch, it is giving out the message that material objects solve problems.

Try instead: When trying to lift children's spirits, don't automatically think of a present as the solution. If practical, suggest taking time together for a special activity – even something as simple as hiding a few (existing, not new!) toys around the garden or house for a mini treasure hunt. If you are pushed for time and have jobs to get done, could you involve the child in them? Make it fun, use a timer, make challenges of chores, and present them as something you can enjoy together to distract from any troubles.

I've seen first-hand how children who have less tend to value their possessions more, and when their rooms and homes are cleared of clutter, they really engage with and enjoy the toys that are left. It's amazing when children walk into their decluttered space for the first time – sometimes around half of their toys will have been removed, yet often one of the first things they say is, 'Wow, look at all my toys!' For the first time they can actually *see* what they have. The clarity that comes from clearing and organising their spaces allows children to thrive.

I find that more and more parents don't need studies and research to tell them that vast hoards of toys are not healthy for their children – quite often the situation gets to a stage where it just doesn't feel right. An increasing number of my bookings are to tackle playrooms, kids' rooms and toy storage in general.

Task 1: Tackling the toy mountain!

Reducing the number of toys in the house is empowering, but don't attempt to purge your child's entire collection at once. The task is too big and you'll feel overwhelmed. Once again, break it down into areas, possibly a cupboard or shelving unit at a time, and follow these simple steps.

1. Have bags for rubbish and charity items ready – and perhaps one for items to pass on.

2. Consider if each toy is age-appropriate. This can be hard when you come across toys that are now too young for your child and they never actually played with them. Guilt may kick in, but don't feel obliged to hang on to items just because of how much you, or someone else, paid for them. If you know that your child is too old for them, then they need to go. Of course, there might be the odd cuddly toy given to your little one as a baby that they still like to cuddle up to, and sentimental items such as these can stay. I don't want any heartbroken children on my conscience! Charity shops and local playgroups will be grateful for any new or good-condition toys. Think how many children can be made happy by your clear-out.

3. Pick up all the random pieces of plastic that seem unrelated to anything. I have lost count of the collections of odd bits and bobs that have been carefully kept by parents in case they are the vital component to some missing kit or toy. If they are lying around, then the chances are the rest of the toy is lost and/or broken anyway. Pop them all in a box, and if, by the end of the process, those bits still don't relate to anything, bin them. Checking through this box of odds and ends is a good job that children can get involved with, they may well know what part fits what toy, and anything that encourages them to be part of the process is a good thing.

4. Avoid duplication. When children tear open a gift only to find it's something they already have, they are often, on principle, still unwilling to let it go – even though they really don't need two. This doesn't just apply to identical toys – take a fresh look at anything which has the same purpose or is very similar to something else. Clearly there are items which children benefit from having several of (particularly puzzles and books), but how many keyboards, toy farms or dolly's pushchairs does one child really need? Now's the time to move on any doubles to homes that will appreciate them.

5. If there really are sets of toys or particular items that you can't bear to get rid of, how about rotating them? Don't complicate things for yourself, just implement a basic rotation which will involve you having a few items that you bring out in the school holidays, for example, when the children are at home more and will appreciate the novelty of having something different to play with. My friend Lucy has her three daughters' Playmobil set (it's pretty extensive – complete with ice-cream parlour!) packed away in a box which she only brings out during the holidays as a special treat – years on, the girls still get so excited! Instead of having something cluttering up daily space, it can be reintroduced at special times and really enjoyed by the children, who don't take it for granted like something they can pick up and put down at any moment.

Applying these steps to all of your toy-storage areas should help you cut down considerably the number of possessions crowding your children's spaces. The process will be so satisfying, and having less to choose from will encourage calm and creativity in them. They will also value more what they have.

Here are a few more tips . . .

Lead by example when decluttering. When clearing out your own possessions make sure your children know and understand what you are doing, especially when you are passing items on to charity, to make others happy. Put a bag or box by their toy storage area and plant the thought that they might like to do the same with some of their belongings . . . watch and wait!

When tackling a big toy box, pick out first the items that you know will definitely be kept. Then pick out the pieces that need to find other components and put them in the bits-and-bobs box (see point 3 above). What's left in the toy box can usually go straight in the bin or to charity, depending on its condition.

If you are worried that your child will find it hard to let go, then involve them in the process, inspire them with a story about the new life that the toys will have. Show no concern on your face, treat the process as entirely normal and you will be surprised at how easy children find it to part with possessions if they can buy into the story of where they are going.

And vitally, never look a teddy in the eye! Your inner child will feel a pang of guilt and you risk doubting your decision to move cuddly toys on, especially the cute ones! I've seen even the strongest adults waver over soft toys.

Task 2: How to store and display toys

Once you've decided what stays and what goes, the key to making sure your children get the most from their toys is in how you store them. I see many homes with complex toy-storage systems – twenty or so labelled boxes, or vast shelving units with countless containers too high for their contents to be seen. Complicated systems do not work. As always, keep it straightforward and follow these tips.

1. Simple cube storage systems, which now come with a great variety of baskets/containers to suit your home and style, are best for keeping toys tidy and organised. There are no lids to trap little fingers and the toys are easy to access for children of all ages and, just as importantly, easy to put away. Keep in these units the toys that you want your little ones to have within reach. When labelling containers, do this clearly in writing that children who are learning to read will be able to decipher for themselves.

2. Children will play with what they can reach. And the more they can reach, the less likely they are to call you every five minutes to fetch something down from a shelf. Again, place at low level anything that you want to encourage them to play with, and enable them to access their toys independently. Imagine that you are your child's height, sit on the floor, move around and see the room through their eyes (yes,

I do this!). What can be pulled down, what looks tempting?

3. Keep heavy items at floor level. This is essential to stop children pulling weighty toys down on top of themselves.

4. Create a 'cosy corner' in your commonly used rooms. However inviting a playroom is, the chances are your child will want to be where you are. So instead of letting them drag a steady stream of toys from the playroom or bedroom into every room in the house, pre-empt this by having a small basket or a couple of storage cubes, preferably on a little rug (a space becomes so much more inviting to children when you place one on a hard floor) in the corner of the kitchen or whichever room you spend most time in. This way you won't end every day picking up bits and bobs scattered all over the house and returning them to the playroom/bedroom.

5. Keep items that you want to restrict use of out of sight. Many households have a daily battle over use of a tablet or games console, but what is out of sight is at least more likely to be out of mind. At times when you don't want technology to be used, store it out of sight and out of temptation's reach. Messy activities that require supervision (such as paints) should also be out of reach. You have far more control over what your children play with than you may think.

6. Encourage the activities that you are passionate about by making them accessible – having a pot of organised pencils and pens with a pad of paper neatly on a table in the playroom makes it easy for children to pick them up and spend time creating. Having the same materials out of sight in a drawer creates a block and means they are less likely to be used.

7. Every child is unique – and so is the way they play. Organise the toys in a way that will make sense for your child by putting things they play with together in the same place. You can also save on storage this way. For example – a friend's children role-play with a whole host of plastic figures of different shapes and sizes. Different characters from various toy sets are all in the mix: Fifi and the Flowertots, Barbie, Postman Pat, Peppa Pig and all their co-stars! All the characters are kept together in one basket, rather than separating them into type or category. A client's child uses toilet rolls as tunnels for his small model cars, so they're all in the same basket rather than having to raid the junk-modelling box for tubes every time he gets the cars out. What I'm saying is how you categorise toys needs to reflect how your children play with them – it doesn't need to make sense to anyone else!

As with all reorganising, the process may not be complete after one hit. In the days and weeks that follow I'm expecting that you'll make tweaks, rearrange where things are and what is in reach, and that is OK. It will become obvious which items are out of place and there will be toys that you notice are still not getting played with, despite being accessible, because they are simply not of interest to your child. These can be moved on. Once you have followed the steps above, talk your children – those who are old enough to understand – through what you have done, explain where things are and that you expect everything to be put away after use. By observing how they play in their decluttered space, you will gain a better understanding of what makes your child tick and – in advance of birthdays and Christmas – you can have a mini clear-out, passing on those items which have not sparked interest. You'll also be able to see clearly and at a glance if there is anything your child needs or would particularly value, and you'll be able to request these when party guests or family ask for gift ideas. Control of the toy situation will once again be yours!

Task 3: How to maintain order (and sanity!)

So you've had the purge, you've sorted out toy storage, and the new organised system is the envy of all the school mums. What could possibly go wrong?! Well, as those with children know, chaos is only one play-date away and from there it's a slippery slope back to playroom anarchy. The key to ensuring that you can maintain order and calm is to get the children on board with tidying up – they need to buy into it so that it becomes second nature, just a part of life, and not a chore.

> ❛ If your child has the motor skills to pick things up and can understand what you're asking, the earlier she does it, the better. It's so much harder to teach good habits later. ❜
>
> Michele Kambolis, *Generation Stressed* (2014)

And, according to Kambolis, it's not just about saving yourself the frustration of having to clean up after your children – by encouraging them to do the job themselves you are actually aiding their development. The mindfulness of the activity develops a key area of the brain (the mid-prefrontal cortex) that's associated with attention span, problem-solving, and mood and body regulation. We all enjoy the pleasure of starting a job, working on it and seeing it to completion. Half-finished tasks provoke anxiety, the key to gaining satisfaction from solving any problem, and it can be as simple as putting toys back in the correct box, is in the completion.

Tidying away toys is also about safety and common sense, the Royal Society for the Prevention of Accidents says toys are involved in more than 40,000 accidents a year. Many of these are caused by people tripping over toys left lying around, particularly on staircases.

But let's not pretend that getting the children to tidy up after themselves is always straightforward – their response can depend on so many factors: how tired they are, how big the task is and whether they are used to putting their things away. Here are a few pointers to help make sure that your organised toy storage can stay that way.

1. Be reasonable. For pre-schoolers our expectations need to be lower than we might think – it's no use asking them to get a whole room in order. Make sure that what you're asking of your child is reasonable, even if it just means getting them to pop five or six toys back in the basket.

2. Lead by example. If your children hear you moaning about constantly having to tidy up then they will soon form the opinion that this is a chore and something to dread and avoid. Instead, tidy up after yourself with no complaint or fuss, demonstrating that this is expected behaviour, no drama involved.

3. Make it fun. Mary Poppins hit the nail on the head when she said: *In every job that must be done, there is an element of fun.* Put music on, race to see who can be the first to put ten things away – if more than one child is involved, adding an element of friendly competition can speed things up. You know your children and you know what makes them tick – use this to your advantage.

4. Help them. At least to start with, hand-holding will be required. By making this an activity you can do with your child, rather than a solitary task for them, you will automatically add to its appeal. This also gives you the chance to make sure it's being done properly! As they get older, the behaviour will become habit and you can take a step back.

5. Set down expectations. For children old enough to understand, explain that if they are intending to empty that *entire* box of farm animals on to the floor, they will have to put them back again when playing is over – and before they empty out another basket! Gentle but firm reminders before play commences that anything taken out will have to be put back avoids nasty surprises for little ones when it comes to tidying up their carnage. It's not about ruining their fun, just making sure that they understand what is expected.

6. Praise them. Rewarding children with praise and commenting on how wonderful a space looks once the toys have been tidied away neatly will encourage them to take pride in their rooms. My nanny training taught me the importance of praise and encouragement and I never underestimate it!

To recap:

> ❛Childhood is not a race to accumulate all of the consumer goods and stresses of adulthood in record time. Simplification signals a change and makes room for transformation. It is a stripping away that invites clarity.❜
>
> Kim John Payne, *Simplicity Parenting*

This 'stripping away' does not have to be a mammoth task. As I've explained here, it can be broken down into areas, each one tackled at your own pace. Once you achieve a level of organisation that works for you, keeping clutter at bay will happen naturally – you will now be mindful of how many toys you allow into the house. Here's a reminder of the key points:

Avoid giving toys as part of your parenting strategies. Think of other ways to reward children, to cheer them up or to compensate for your lack of time with them, or as a response to peer pressure.

Limit the gifts received – at least take control of what comes into the house at Christmas and birthdays by giving suggestions for present ideas that will be useful or that are experiences rather than possessions.

Tackle each toy-storage area at a time. Take on one shelving unit, one toy box. This way you can break the job down.

Move on toys that are not age-appropriate, uninteresting to your children, broken, or have parts missing or are duplicated.

Rotate. For sets of toys that you want to keep, consider boxing them up to be brought out at certain times so that they continue to be valued.

Use straightforward systems like cube storage to encourage children to tidy up.

Keep things within reach. Make sure that little hands can safely and easily reach what they need, and put out of reach/sight those items which you want to restrict use of.

Store and arrange toys to suit your child. Consider what they play with most and cater the storage for their individual needs.

Encourage tidying up: lead by example – avoid moaning about your own chores, make it fun, help when needed, have clear and reasonable expectations and reward with praise.

Transforming a child's bedroom or playroom into a sanctuary in which they can relax, be creative and play is one of the most rewarding examples of how decluttering and organising can transform lives. You've now read about my theory and my methods, and with these at your disposal I know you can make this happen for your children.

7

Home Offices and Paperwork

When it comes to the causes of clutter, piles of paperwork are high on my list of offenders. They pop up everywhere. Look around you, I bet there is one in sight . . .

As these piles get higher, bills are paid late, important documents are lost and getting on top of the paperwork feels like an impossible task. When our filing is out of control, we feel out of control – it's as simple as that. Sherrie Bourg Carter, author of *High Octane Women: How Superachievers Can Avoid Burnout* (2010), recognises how disorganisation in our paperwork can affect our productivity:

❝ Clutter distracts us by drawing our
attention away from what our focus should be
on ... It frustrates us by preventing us from
locating what we need quickly, e.g. files
and paperwork lost in the "pile". ❞

Having a streamlined system for sorting out your home admin can take such a weight off your mind, yet so many people put the task off and suffer because of it. My methods for filing all of your paperwork and dealing with post are, as always, practical and straightforward. In fact they are so straightforward that often a client's biggest hurdle is getting over the fear of such simplicity! Complicated systems are frequently mistaken for organised ones.

The key benefits of having an organised filing system

Taking back control

We all know the feeling when you can't lay your hands on the right form or you lose an invitation or important piece of paperwork. As well as being annoyed and frustrated with yourself, you feel out of control. Disorganised. You become reactive rather than proactive, responding to everything at the last minute because the right documents aren't to hand, over-committing socially because you've lost track of where you are supposed to be and when, forking out penalties because you're late paying bills. It all adds to that drowning feeling. Putting simple systems in place for your paperwork that are easy to implement and keep up allows you to control your admin and your schedule, not the other way around.

Having more mental energy

Worrying can be exhausting – it leaves us feeling drained. How many times have you woken up in a cold sweat fretting about where your passport is or if you have renewed your home insurance? Being organised with your filing means spending less time in fear that you might forget or lose something; it gets rid of that nagging feeling and replaces it with clarity. It means less time spent on home admin, and that can only be a good thing, right?

Saving money

Late payments and losing track of direct debits are such a common problem in so many households. There is of course no need for it when there is a clear, follow-able solution. Once you gain the clarity of organised paperwork you will have the headspace to get on top of everything else.

Managing time well

If every minute that is meant to be 'you time' is spent catching up on paperwork and admin, then your current system isn't working. The systems I implement are designed to make it very clear in your mind how much you have to get through, as well as taking the effort away from tasks like filing that are usually dreaded.

The secret of efficient filing!

When Vicky explained what we were going to do to get my paperwork straight I must admit I was doubtful that it could work, thinking, *This is way too simple to work for me*. Vicky could tell I was hesitant and we talked it through. Sure enough, it is now working like a dream! I had been over-complicating my life and wasting my time for years!

Steve, 45

People often associate filing with having to put complicated systems in place – this couldn't be further from the truth! We all have so many documents, forms and so on coming our way every week that the secret to filing them efficiently is to keep it as simple as possible.

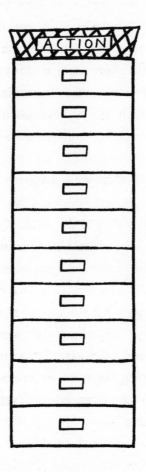

I began implementing this system around ten years ago when I was a PA and I've had so much positive feedback on it – it works for everyone and makes such a difference to people's lives. Feeling organised at home is empowering, if we feel up to date and on top of things, we face challenges with confidence.

If we have to ponder over every piece of paper, find the hole-punch, punch holes in it, reach a folder down from a shelf and flick through subject dividers to find where it goes, put it in the right place, put the folder back, put the hole-punch away, then it's just not going to happen! All these stages are a further example of what I call 'blocks' – obstacles in your way of getting the job done. Subconsciously you are aware of these stages, and when you glance at the paperwork instead of filing it you're likely to be put off by the hurdles in your way and set it aside to deal with another day. Before you know it, a pile of papers has built up, and instead of a two-minute job you're looking at thirty minutes to sort through the lot. That's time you don't have, so it doesn't happen.

Getting started: what you need

A filing cabinet of drawers – not hanging files, but shallower drawers in which the paperwork lies flat. I highly recommend the Bisley 10- or 15-drawer cabinet. Depending on your paperwork you might need more than one, but this is usually enough for family and household paperwork. The cabinet should live either in the room you do your paperwork in or somewhere between there and the front door.

A4 paperwork storage boxes with lids.

An open A4-size paperwork tray.

A few A4 thumb-cut plastic folders (the ones with two sides sealed and two open).

A bag for recycling and one for shredding.

From now on *any* piece of paperwork that comes into your home will only have one of two places to live:

Action Pile: If you need to do something/anything with it, then it lives here until it's done.

File: If you need to keep it but there is no action required, it gets posted straight into one of your neatly labelled drawers

It really is that simple.

Though the system itself is straightforward, however, as with most tasks, it does involve some preparation. As usual, I've broken the job down for you into achievable chunks.

Categorise

It's time to say goodbye to your existing filing system (which may just consist of random piles!) and to establish what categories you need for the labels on your new drawers. You are about to get yourself organised!

If you have any concerns that there are only 10–15 drawers, then please know that I understand every family is different, with different needs and situations. But this really can be sufficient for the basics of everyday living. I have seen so on many occasions.

So back to the main paperwork blitz. This is how it goes . . .

1. Make sure you have a large clear area of floor in the room in which you are working.

2. Have bags ready for rubbish and recycling.

3. You are going to start by gathering every single piece of paperwork you can find around your home and getting it into one area.

4. Lay each piece of paper on the floor in its category (see the list on page 132) and arrange the piles in neat straight lines. In front of each pile put a Post-it note with the category written on it. The key is to keep categories broad and simple.

5. Put any items that need actioning – vouchers to spend, bills to pay, school notes to return – together in one pile with a Post-it note marked 'Action'.

6. You will probably come across old paperwork, perhaps going back years. Recycle or shred anything that doesn't need to be kept. If it does need to be kept for financial reasons it can go in a separate box marked 'Archive'. Label clearly the contents of the box. I have some clients who not only don't have the space to store this paperwork but who also like to scan documents and archive them electronically instead. Scanning takes time so don't view this as a necessity – otherwise, paperwork will yet again become a time-consuming chore that you will put off tackling. It's often easier to pop the relevant document into your archive box and store it outside your living space.

7. Put guarantees, bulky manuals and instructions for appliances in neat piles, and label. It is a good idea to split these into three categories: e.g., kids, kitchen and general. Check through all of them to see if they are still relevant. Many instruction manuals are now available online, which saves more space, but if like me you prefer an easily accessible visual record, store in one of your A4 boxes, neatly labelled.

8. If you are doing this when time is short and you need to stop, then put each pile into one of your thumb-cut folders, easily and quickly clearing the floor space until you're able to resume.

The floor should now be covered in neat piles all clearly labelled! You can now bin those bulky files and lever-arch folders – they are not part of your filing system any more.

By now the categories that you need to label for your drawer cabinet should be becoming clear from the piles that you have put together. Anything that needs to be separated within a drawer can be placed in a thumb-cut file.

Every family is different, but here are some suggested categories for your drawers, most of which will be applicable to the average household:

Important documents (you may prefer to keep this drawer unlabelled for security reasons).

Passports, driving licence, any visa documents, marriage and birth certificates, wills, forms of ID etc.

Household bills

Utility, phone bills, TV licence etc.

Car

MOT certificate, insurance docs, service history, vehicle registration details, recovery schemes etc.

House/mortgage

Up-to-date insurance for buildings, home and contents, current mortgage

Pension and life insurance

Medical/health

Any health-insurance documents and medical records. If anyone in your family has ongoing health issues then this may need to be split between drawers; if not, then one drawer can suffice for a whole family. Children's red books, NHS numbers and so on go here.

Travel

Holiday booking details, ideas, air miles or similar travel points schemes, travel insurance details.

Bank accounts

Statements, annual interest summaries etc.

Credit cards and store cards

Statements and bills etc.

Stocks, shares, investments

Tax/accountancy documents

Memberships

Gym, National Trust subscriptions etc.

These are just options that might be useful – every household has different filing needs. Some of my clients like to save magazine cuttings for a fun project, or interior-decorating ideas, recipes and so on. I think that these should be separate from daily filing and kept in A4 boxes so that they are portable. Boxes such as these represent your interests, they're a fun thing, which is why I would keep this kind of material away from your cabinet. The box can be picked up one evening so that you can have a rummage through in the lounge to find the recipe or article you need.

Having all of your important documents together means that you can easily lay your hands on them and that you will always have somewhere clear and obvious to put them away. There is no need to separate utility bills you will rarely look at but, providing you pop them in the drawer as they arrive, if you do need to look through them they will naturally be in date order.

The best bit!

And here comes the most satisfying part! Once you have decided on your categories and completed your labels, it's time to pop each pile into the relevant drawer. This system offers total ease, practicality and speed and now that it's up and running I know that you'll love it! Over time as drawers become full, for financial matters (banking etc.), for instance, simply move the paperwork into an archive box – loft or attic is fine, anywhere out of the way of your living space – otherwise, it can be recycled or shredded.

How long do I need to keep paperwork for?

Previously we were told that you only need to keep bank, credit card and other personal finance documents for six years. (This is because the taxman can only ask you to go back that far if you're being investigated for tax purposes.) However, Martin Lewis of moneysavingexpert. com now recommends holding on to it for as long as possible. This is in case you need to claim money back due to the mis-selling of financial packages such as PPI.

> Evidence of systemic mis-selling often takes years to work through the system – if it's related to a pension it could be many decades. So, it's impossible now to say what you may need the paperwork for in a few years' time. Therefore, for safety, keeping old documents as long as you can – even for now-closed products – is a reasonable precaution.
>
> Martin Lewis

This does not give you permission to be lazy with your paperwork and to stash it away in a disorganised state. I suggest you keep only your annual statements and clear records of any interest or fees paid. This is not an excuse to keep every piece of paper! And remember, these old records do not need to be in your daily space – put them in the archive boxes which can then be stored out of the way.

Your action pile

The words 'to do' (regarding either a pile or a list) have always grated on me. Maybe it goes back to the ten years of continuous admin I did when I was a PA! For me 'actioning' something is far more positive and dynamic than simply just 'doing', so let's call that pile of paperwork that you need to work through your action pile. This should be kept in a single open-top filing tray, preferably on top of, or very near to, your filing cabinet.

Go around the house and collect those stray documents that you have been meaning to do something with: that order for those school photos, or the gift voucher you put away somewhere random. Pop them all in the tray. From now on you will know where everything that requires action is, and whenever you have time to do some admin you can flick through it and pull out your priority items. I don't like to prescribe set time slots that you should allocate to admin, everyone's schedule is different. With such a simple system to follow you will be able to chip away at the action pile, little and often, without filing having to become a chore which encroaches on your free time.

Now that your paperwork is organised you will find many items that require action are less daunting and more satisfying to complete. For example, how many times have you put off filling in an application form or similar because it requires proof of ID and you have no idea where your passport is? Knowing that you can quickly and easily lay your hands on your driving licence and other documents makes many other tasks feel more achievable.

When it comes to your paperwork, really, there is no need to be writing 'to do' lists. The pile is your list! However, I know many avid list writers and I also know that making a written note helps many people feel in control. For lists to be effective and to avoid them becoming part of the clutter ensure they are kept in one place. At the end of a busy day put your notebook on the top of your action pile. This is its new home!

Take note! A word of warning on notepads

Notebooks are like plastic bags – people seem to end up with masses of them! Take it from me, when you are feeling disorganised buying a notebook (or other stationery) is not the solution – you're just adding to the clutter at home. And having more than one notebook on the go at once is asking for trouble – you'll forget which one that vital note or number is in, and pick up the wrong one in haste. You're making your life more, not less, complicated!

To recap:

Invest in the following: A 10- or 15-drawer cabinet (more than one, if needed), A4 storage boxes with lids, archive boxes, one paper tray for your action pile, plastic thumb-cut folders for anything that you need to separate out within a drawer.

Sort your paperwork into neat piles on a clear surface (usually the floor) in basic categories.

Shred or recycle old or irrelevant paperwork at the end of this task, not as you're going along. In future shredding *can* be done as you go along.

Group smaller subjects together (e.g. all utility bills) and label your drawers according to your piles.

Put older documentation that you need to store in a box labelled 'archive'.

Put warranties, instructions, manuals etc. into labelled boxes.

Post each pile in the relevant drawer (you'll love this bit!)

Put anything which requires your attention on the action pile.

I guarantee that you will achieve an incredible sense of satisfaction once this system is up and running. It really is as simple as it sounds – no catches, just a set of drawers and one action tray.

Clarity and efficiency (and smugness!) are now yours!

8

The Kitchen

Mornings in my kitchen were where the stress started. The rushing around, making lunches, trying to gulp down a cup of tea ... all such simple tasks until children are involved! My cupboards were jammed and surfaces stuffed, there wasn't really any logic to anything. Vicky and her team transformed it. They showed me how to make simple changes that have had a massive effect. Now the morning routine runs smoothly and I leave the house feeling in control. I can't believe how such simple tips have made such a difference to how I start the day.

Emma, 37

So many of us, like Emma, begin the day on a bad note and – as we know – a stressful start often sets the tone for the whole day. Clutter breeds clutter and having a disorganised kitchen makes it hard for us to lay our hands on everyday items, which only adds to the pressure when we are already pushed for time. How many of us leave for work having hurriedly closed the front door on a scene more akin to feeding time at the zoo than a family breakfast? The image of the chaos that we leave behind stays with us through the day and this is the scene we will return home to. The day has barely begun and we already feel overwhelmed.

With some simple changes to the set-up of your kitchen, I promise that the morning rush can run smoothly! Imagine leaving your house feeling in a state of control rather than chaos. If your day has begun with order, then I believe your mood will be positive and your productivity levels high. And whatever the day throws at you, it is comforting to know that you have your oasis of calm to return to when it is over.

Every house or flat is different but the kitchen is usually the hub of the home – meals are prepared (and often eaten) here, food and drink (and secret snacks!) stored here, homework is completed, endless cups of tea are consumed and it's the place where family and friends gather together. This is the room with the most traffic, and such heavy-duty usage requires a practical, methodical approach to layout and storage. My clients are always surprised at how small tweaks can have a big impact on how their kitchen functions for them. As with my approach to all rooms and spaces, decluttering and organising your kitchen needs to be broken down into manageable tasks that can be done when you have twenty or thirty minutes to spare.

If you were to try and tackle the room as a whole, the kitchen would be out of action for a whole day, possibly a lot longer. Attempting to reorganise such a busy space all at once also means you run the risk of either running out of steam or having to stop mid-way through if you are interrupted. A client with small children said she'd attempted to declutter her kitchen three times before giving up, as on each occasion she had to stop halfway through because of other demands on her time.

Change doesn't have to happen overnight; small steps make a difference and quickly produce results. After all, how long have you put this off for already?

So, in simple stages, let's get started!

Task 1: Fresh eyes

Equipment needed: Just you, this is your starting point!

First, leave your kitchen. Shut the door and take a deep breath. When you walk back in, you are going to look at the room in a new way. Scan from left to right, open all the cupboards and drawers, assess the room as a whole and ask yourself 'Does this make sense?' Some things to ask yourself:

Are the items you need to access daily in easy-to-reach places?

Is cupboard space being taken up by things that you hardly ever use?

Are you walking around the kitchen five times just to make a cup of tea?

Do you have too many of one thing?

Do you have items/appliances that you never use?

When looking at all of your storage space, try to be realistic as you make a mental log of what might need to either move around or leave your home for good. Filling up prime storage spots with rarely used crockery or glasses but cramming the coffee cups you use every day in an overcrowded corner cupboard makes no sense. Peer into every cupboard, even the hard-to-access ones under the breakfast bar or the small cupboard above the fitted fridge-freezer. Don't be tempted to start moving items around yet – this task is all about assessing, action comes later!

Once you have a feel for all those forgotten/barely used possessions that are taking up your precious space you should be raring to get started.

Task 2: Getting started

Equipment needed: Plastic storage boxes, labels and a chubby black pen

Let's start by freeing up some space in your kitchen and making it more practical. Remove any items that you only need at either certain times of the year or every now and then. I call these 'occasional ware'. Dinner-party serving plates, 'best' crockery or glasses and BBQ tools are among items that I often find taking up daily space in clients' kitchens. If you have spaces in your kitchen that are less accessible, you might have room for these boxes there, but the chances are you'll have to house them elsewhere – perhaps in the garage or an under-stairs cupboard. Basically they need to live somewhere that you will only need to access every so often.

I choose sturdy plastic boxes with handles that click into place and close tightly. These are storage investments and will probably be in your life for years, so don't scrimp and buy poor-quality versions or you'll end up having to get more when they inevitably break! With your labels and marker pens at the ready, fill these boxes by category. These will probably include:

Posh cutlery sets

Your best crockery

Large serving dishes

Fondue sets, popcorn makers and other rarely used gadgets

Barbecue tools

Before you place items in the boxes, ask yourself: Will I use this again? Is it in good condition and do I know if it works? If the answer to any of these questions is 'no', then do not store the item. Get rid of it! You could consider passing items on to friends or family who might find them useful, but be wary of turning up unannounced at friends' houses with boxes full of your unwanted belongings – people often find it hard to say 'no' when put on the spot and you will have simply shifted the clutter from your house to theirs. They won't thank you for that! Make sure that any items you do decide to pass on leave your house as soon as possible. It is easy to fall into the trap of having boxes allocated to other people cluttering up your hall, but it's time to be ruthless. Prioritise your need to create order above re-homing your belongings to friends. This is your time, your space, your project.

Once the boxes are packed, clearly label them and put them in their new home. Labels will stop you forgetting the contents in the future. You should now have more kitchen space for the items you use daily. Seeing the benefit of this simple task should whet your appetite for more action when your next spare moment arises!

Task 3: Clear the decks

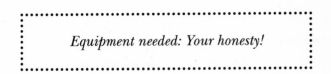

Equipment needed: Your honesty!

Now that you've packed away those rarely used items, it's time to give storage priority to the bits and bobs that you need to lay your hands on quickly and easily every day. To do this, you need to be honest about what kind of cook you are . . . not what kind of cook you'd like to be!

Are you a smoothie junkie or a nifty Nigella in the kitchen? Are you queen of the ready meals or a demon with your dicer? In our ideal worlds we are probably all prancing around in aprons blending organic squash for the little ones and baking masterpieces to wow our friends. In reality, we're decanting brand-name orange mush from jars and sprinkling icing sugar over shop-bought sponges for that home-baked look! Do you see where I'm going with this?

If you rarely use your food processor, take it off the kitchen worktop where it is a dust magnet and place it in a low cupboard. Ideally, choose one cupboard to keep all of these items together so you know where they are. (I recommend lower cupboards for anything heavy.) This also goes for all the flash bits of kit that take up valuable space and spend more time as ornaments than appliances.

If you're a whizz in the kitchen you will need a variety of tools and kit in your daily space, but if, like lots of us, you hardly ever have time to cook completely from scratch, then what are you doing with a pestle and mortar as a permanent feature on your worktop? All I'm saying is, be realistic. I'm not trying to crush your dreams of culinary genius.

As you go through the kitchen you may come across that juicer you bought during a health kick. Why not give it a trial run in a prime position, to prompt yourself to use it? Give it a week and if you still haven't used it, it goes!

Which utensils take the top spot?

Pour all your utensils out of the drawer/holder, lay them all out in front of you on a clear surface and pick out the ones you definitely use. If you do a moderate amount of cooking you will know which tools you use frequently and these should be within easy reach, either in a holder on the worktop or in a utensils drawer located near your hob/cooker. As for the rest, ask yourself if you are really ever going to have a use for them? Isn't it time to move the melon ball scoop on (so very Eighties!) and the avocado slicer? Make sure your kitchen contains the essentials relevant to *your* lifestyle, not anyone else's.

As well as ditching the quirky gadgets that take up drawers and worktop space, take a fresh look at the clutter that fills your cupboards. The following articles are lurking

within all of our kitchens and are often useful to keep, but not worthy of a prime spot. Let's think of them as top-shelf items, because that's where they should be kept.

Egg cups

Gravy boats

Tea pots (be honest, how often do you bother? Just when Granny comes round?)

Giant saucepans

Remember, most cupboards have adjustable shelving, so change them to suit your needs and make the best use of your precious space. This is a simple change that makes a big difference in streamlining your kitchen.

Task 4: Fancy a cuppa?

Hang on, while I just stroll to the other side of the kitchen for a tea bag, then back to the far corner for a mug. Over to the fridge for milk and bear with me as I rummage for a teaspoon in a drawer at the opposite end of the kitchen . . . and then back to the kettle. (And don't ask for sugar, that's somewhere in a canister at the back of a cupboard.)

Do you get the picture? Many of my clients say that mornings are such a struggle that they often leave the house without having had time for a cuppa. When your kitchen is not set up to make everyday tasks straightforward and it is bustling with people, everyone in a rush, then the simplest tasks can seem impossible. If, like me, you need a morning brew to kick-start the day, then make it easy for yourself and set up a tea and coffee station. Allocate a cupboard above your kettle and use it to house your teas, coffees and hot chocolates, with a neighbouring shelf for your mugs. If your cutlery drawer is not conveniently placed below, take a few teaspoons and put them in a pretty jar in the same cupboard. You will be surprised what a difference having everything within easy reach for your cuppa makes!

Task 5: A happy, healthy fridge

> *Equipment needed: Clear storage boxes or large jars*

It was New Year and I decided it was time to start a new health regime. Vicky helped me declutter my kitchen but when it came to my fridge I didn't really think she could make a difference. But wow, she really did! All my healthy food now lives on one shelf and it's the first thing I see every morning. My neat and tidy fridge inspires me to eat healthily and to keep track of what food needs eating up.

Becca, 28

Most of us do our food shop in a hurry and often without having even written a list. Yes, we all know that it would only take a minute to scribble one down, but that's a minute we don't have! How many times, though, do you get home to find you already have the things you thought you needed, lurking at the back of the fridge, and those items you thought you had plenty of are about to run out? And how many of us face the guilt of throwing out entire packets of food that have been festering at the back of the fridge as their use-by date has come and gone? It's a horrible feeling – no one wants to be wasteful.

For this task, here are some pointers on making your fridge your friend and saving on waste!

Clear out shelf by shelf. Take out, on to a clear surface, all the jars of relish and so on that are cluttering up your fridge. If any are past their use-by dates, bin them. Wipe down each shelf – starting with a clean space inspires us to use it efficiently and you have a blank canvas to start with.

Replace at eye level the food you want to eat most of. If you're trying to eat more healthily, then make sure your fresh fruit and vegetables are the first things you see when you open the fridge. (And hide the chocolate as much as possible.)

Store food items you'd like children to have access to at the lowest possible height. This might involve creating their own area so that items they are allowed to help themselves to are within easy reach, and then placing the 'treats' higher up or hidden away. Allowing children to help themselves to their snacks from the fridge is one less reason for them to holler for your help getting something they can't reach!

Pre-chop salad items or veg for roasting. When your shopping first arrives, how about blitz-chopping salad and veg and popping them in transparent containers such as large glass jars. This will make meal preparation for the next few days much easier and means you are much more likely to use them up before they go off.

Make the most of flexible storage. Remember you can often move refrigerator shelves up and down. So adjust to suit what you are storing so as to ensure you don't have any dead space.

Task 6: Geek up your cupboards

Equipment needed: No unnecessary gimmicky storage

Let's go through the basics, and I'll keep this advice as clear and straightforward as your food cupboards should be!

Food should be stored in cupboards in categories: tinned, dried, sauces, snacks and so on.

Create a breakfast cupboard containing all spreads and cereals. (Remember the rule about moving shelves for those tall cereal boxes.) If you have children old enough to start making their own breakfast, why not make sure this cupboard is within their reach and encourage them to serve themselves?

Store your most-used cooking oils, sauces, vinegars etc. in a cupboard next to your hob for easy access while cooking.

Store 'goodies' and snacks in a basket (or two!) within a cupboard. This snack box can then be easily grabbed for dishing goodies out to the little monsters.

Don't be tempted to bulk-buy if you haven't got room for storage. You'll end up with overflowing cupboards and will actually waste more if you can't see clearly what you have and what needs eating up.

If you have a drawer free by the end of this declutter, spice jars work well when laid on their side for easy viewing. Alternatively, pop them in a shallow basket in a cupboard.

Remember: whether you're organising a wardrobe, cupboard or kitchen, the same rule applies: if you can't see it, you don't use it. This is especially true of food. If cupboards are cluttered you won't be able to see many of their contents, so keep it simple and organised – don't bulk-buy or cram shelves full.

A few last words on the kitchen

Because it is the heart of your home, having a wonderfully organised kitchen will enhance your life more than you expect. Think of this room as mission HQ for your day: you feed the troops here, dispatch them (with their supplies) from here and hold your daily briefing here (over a morning cuppa). Alongside completing the tasks above, follow these tips to help you get the streamlined kitchen that works *for* you, not against you. You won't be disappointed – I promise!

Make sure you give all cupboards a good wipe out before placing items back in. You want that fresh, clean, completed feeling.

Keep the area on top of kitchen cupboards clear, to avoid a cluttered look. Having items stored overhead can make the room feel overwhelming and oppressive.

Tell the family about the changes you have made and give them a tour. This will also help you avoid a million 'Where is it?' questions!

Before emptying cupboards and drawers, make sure you have a large clear area to lay the contents out on. Whether it's a kitchen table or your work surface, use this area to categorise items. You need to see clearly what you have.

Don't go out and buy a range of containers and gizmos for kitchen storage. We often need very little other than the cupboards and drawers themselves. There's no need to make it complicated. The only thing I usually add to kitchens is a range of plastic baskets, but to use only as and when needed.

Don't throw away food that's in date – give it to a food bank instead. (See page 195 for information on how to find a bank near you.)

Think cleverly when buying new sets of products – there are ranges of saucepans and plastic food-storage containers that can be stored within each other.

Don't double up on cleaning products – stick to a few that do the job. I often see clients' under-sink cupboards crammed full with crazy quantities of glass cleaner, sprays and disinfectants! The shops aren't going to sell out so buy as and when you need.

Don't worry if you move things around several times – the kitchen is a tricky area to get right first time. As you use it over the days following your sort-out, you will be able to spot any tweaks that need to be made.

If you complete these tasks and start afresh with a place for everything it will be easier than you think to keep up the good work. It's all about a friendly level of organisation – you'll love it!

9

Living Spaces and Everywhere Else!

You come home from work, kick off your shoes and sink into your sofa to de-stress after a hectic day ... only, it doesn't quite work because the room is full of clutter which you should be tackling. Sounds familiar? I know how much I value moments of stillness (however brief!) in my own living room – lighting a candle after a busy day, enjoying the calm of a well-ordered space. Having this sanctuary to return to is essential for my wellbeing. Imagine if you could enjoy the same feeling and if, instead of glancing around with a sense of rising panic at the disorder, you could truly relax, guilt-free in your own home.

In this chapter I'll cover all the areas of a living space that commonly need organising, and there is also an element of retraining your brain here. These parts of the house are the most likely areas in which you will dump and discard belongings, so now you need to get into the simple habit of making every journey within your home as effortlessly productive as possible. This means carrying something with you every time you go upstairs: as you walk to your child's room to put clean clothes away also pick up a toy or two on your way; or as you leave the lounge, look around for magazines or newspapers that you can take out and put with the recycling. Combine a little tidying with each of your primary tasks.

The hallway

Before you make it onto the sofa, you've probably had to turn a blind eye to the clutter that greeted you as you walked through your front door. The sight of coats and shoes everywhere is not the 'Welcome home' that any of us need. Hallways will always be dumping grounds, there's nothing you can do about that – we walk through the door and instinctively want to shed the clobber of the day. Coat hooks are overloaded, shoe storage is piled high and discarded bags litter the floor. Mail is picked up and hurriedly put on the nearest available surface.

My suggestion

If storage for the items that we tend to throw off as we enter the front door is anywhere other than in the hallway, then the chances are they will not get put away – they'll stay put on the floor or chucked over a chair, at the exact spot where they were taken off. It's unrealistic to expect anyone, on entering the home, to traipse around putting their bag, shoes and coat in different locations. For storage to be used effectively it needs to be to hand, where it is most needed. I recommend the following:

At least one coat hook per family member, with children's hooks positioned lower down so that they can hang up their own jackets. If you have room for more hooks, then go for it. Better to have the coats spread out over a longer row than having many piled on top of one hook. Over time, the bulge of all these coats will slowly encroach into the hallway, dropping off one by one every time you brush past them.

Invest in a practical statement piece and make a feature of storage. Space is often tight in hallways but if you have room for an armoire or cupboard, this is the perfect solution for storing coats tidily away – bags too, if the hanging space allows them to be placed underneath. I have a client who actually knocked a small space from her hallway to her lounge to make a coat cupboard – she saw this as a priority. The hallway had become a dumping ground and, after one trip-up too many over the piles on the floor, she decided to make the investment and get the builders in! If this is an area that really bothers you, then sacrificing a small amount of space in the next room to create a hall storage cupboard could be a worthwhile option.

Use simple flat shelves for shoe storage. As mentioned in Chapter Five, I've seen some terrible racks in my time – they've become my pet hate! Don't use anything with an angled shelf or made from flimsy wire-racking, as shoes slide off or fall through holes, especially in a hallway where all it will take is a slight bump from someone passing to knock everything off. Ideally, use a large sturdy shelving unit with adjustable shelves for shoe storage. Winter boots take up more space, so in the summer you want to be able to adjust the shelves and avoid a mass of dead space. Face shoes forward for an ordered look.

Only use hall shoe storage for the shoes that you wear daily. Seasonal and occasionally worn footwear belongs in bedrooms.

Have an open intray (not one with several slots) as near to the front door as possible. Place it vertically (i.e. fixed to the wall) or horizontally, depending on the space you have. Post should be neatly put in here, and only here, before being moved on to be dealt with.

Don't just use under-stairs cupboards as a dumping ground. If utilised properly, this space can work really well for you because, although they may be awkward in shape, these cupboards are usually quite deep. Think of what you most lack storage for and look at the space available. If it is a viable option, this is an area worth some investment – why not get some bespoke built-in storage? With the help of a carpenter you could create a space kitted out exactly to suit your needs.

Books

I love books and still feel you can't beat holding a 'real' book – enjoying it, finishing it . . . and then passing it on for someone else to enjoy. But I know that not all avid readers feel the same, and that many people are fiercely protective of their books. They love having them lined up on shelves, being able to glance at each spine and recall the pleasure that particular read gave them. To those clients who are resistant to letting go of books, I always ask, *When was the last time you did this? And when was the last time you reread any of these books?*

If every space in your home is vital, then I know that you'll benefit so much from moving part of your collection on. I have clients who have built shelf after shelf to house their books until it feels like their walls are closing in on them. (And actually, they are!) As I have said before, think of your home as a giant box that is slowly getting filled. If we don't part with some of our possessions there is only one outcome! We have to prioritise what we choose to keep by deciding not only what is important to us, but also what is useful, what we actually need. Make the decision to live with less rather than just having a declutter. It can be a far more powerful mindset to adopt.

My suggestion

I have many clients who start the day saying, 'Oh no, I won't be getting rid of any books.' And yet when I encourage them, just to humour me, to glance at the spines quickly from left to right, a 'charity pile' always emerges. Even the most fanatical readers tend to dispense with at least fifteen to twenty books, creating some wonderful and usually much-needed space.

Getting back even a small amount of space can be all it takes to get a client going. It's like it kicks them into action – suddenly they surprise themselves and know they can keep the good work up.

Here's how to approach your book collection:

As always, start with a clear surface and then pull all of your books down on to it from where they are living. Lift them down in batches placing them on their sides, spines facing upwards, so you can easily see the titles. Don't focus on any specific books yet.

From left to right, glance through and pull out any that you instantly know you don't need in your life/will not reread or didn't particularly like anyway. Books take up so much space, so if you are struggling for it in your home and want to live more clearly, let as many go as you can, knowing they could make someone else very happy. Unless you really feel passionate about them, why are you hanging on to them? Just in case you decide to read them again? How likely is that? Because all these 'just in case' books are taking up a lot of space in your home for something that may or may not happen.

Step back and enjoy the space that you see on the empty shelves, just for a second or two. How useful could that space be to you? How much do you value it? These books are renting your space – are they worthy of it?

*

When my mum was in hospital back in 2012 my brothers, Nick and Jamie, and I visited her frequently. I remember seeing an elderly lady in the next bed staring into space – no visitors and a pile of books by her side. I asked if I could pass her one as they were out of reach. She told me that she had read them all, so I asked if I could get her one from the library trolley and she told me that she had read all those as well. My heart totally sank. A lady with nothing to do, no visitors, she'd been in there for weeks and now not even a book to read. It broke my heart. That night my brothers and I gathered some unread, unloved books from home that had been gathering dust on shelves for years and we took them to her the following day. Her face said it all. So simple, no hard work involved, just a small amount of thought.

The items you give to charity all end up with a new story. A new life. They all go on to a new home. Sometimes we just have to use our imagination to appreciate how happy our unused 'stuff' can make others.

Hospital wards and care homes are often grateful for well-kept books. It only takes a quick phone call to check if your nearest one needs any. Think how many people would love to have their often stale library refreshed. Again, how many people could you make happy?

Anyway, back to *your* books.

Once you have limited your book collection to those that you can really afford the space for, then it's time to think about how best to display them. A wall of books can look like a work of art if they are arranged in a way that is neat and not chaotic, but how you do this is a matter of personal taste. I would divide my book-loving clients into two groups: those who view books mainly as a decorative design feature, often arranged by colour, and those who like them arranged by genre.

DVDs and CDs

You would be amazed at the number of clients I come across who have boxes or shelves of DVDs, CDs and even videos but no longer have a DVD or CD player – and definitely not a VHS player! So many of us now stream our films and music, which is obviously great from a simple-living perspective – less clutter filling our homes. If we still insist on keeping the CDs and DVDs so that we can, one day, download the content from them, then we are losing the benefit that this wonderful space-saving technology offers. Rows of CDs or DVDs on shelves just don't have the same visual appeal as books and often end up looking messy, so the sooner you can part with them and free up the space the better.

My suggestion

If you feel nostalgic about your CD collection (we all have certain songs that take us back to different periods of our lives), then remember that by moving the physical item on you are not saying goodbye to the music – it's still out there, downloadable at any time! You are simply saying goodbye to the disc that is holding it. And if a track or album is special to you, surely you will already have downloaded it? Holding on to the hard copy is just doubling up.

Take a closer look and consider how many of your CDs represent phases or music fads and tastes that you are just not into any more – they can go without hesitation! If you are adamant that you will convert the CDs into digital format, put a few of your favourites aside – chances are you will not get around to it, but limiting what you keep to a small selection means the task is less daunting, should you have the time. Sadly, despite the money that we may have forked out at the time, CDs are worth a relatively small amount now, so if you are intending to sell them, it's important to find a way that is quick and easy. There are some great websites (see page 195 for my recommendation) that buy old CDs and allow you to check the value of your collection on their website, follow their instructions for boxing up your CDs and then pop them in the post – some even offer free postage. The websites will then pay the money direct into your bank account. Just be realistic about this and think about giving yourself a time limit to get it done.

Ornaments

Ornaments – love them or hate them, I bet you have a few lying about the place. If candles, knick-knacks and photos are all fighting for space it creates an overwhelming feeling of clutter. Walking into a room where every shelf and surface is crowded with belongings immediately gives an untidy impression and a feeling of disorder. From a boring and practical point of view, ornaments are also dust magnets!

Take a fresh look at the items on your shelf, remembering that, when it comes to appreciating ornaments, less is definitely more. I have a beautiful, colourful little vase that my mum gave to me and I realised one day that it was lost among a sea of other bits and bobs. Once I cleared and reorganised that shelf, the vase stood out in all its glory. Precious photos and mementos worth keeping should be visible, and that means cutting out the stuff that surrounds them.

Photos

Photos are one of my *favourite* things. I am passionate about photography (albeit in an amateur way). I absolutely love looking through old photos and often bring a box out when family or friends are visiting. The method I use to store mine not only takes up very little of my time but is easy and enjoyable too. I hate *only* having photos stored in digital format. Retrieving photos from old laptops and redundant mobile phones used to be an ongoing task in my action pile. I still sometimes wonder if years of precious photos have been lost, left on computers I no longer have . . . but I certainly don't let it bother me, as there's nothing I can do about it now. However, the solution I found was to embrace a bit of simple-to-use modern technology. I now have a method that suits me perfectly because, personally, I like to feel a photograph in my hand. Glancing at each print one by one, each one a different memory.

Like most of us I take the majority of photographs on my phone. There are wonderful apps (see page 195 for my favourites) which mean you simply set up an account, click on your images, choose the size you'd like and a few days later they arrive on your doorstep! This for me is as exciting as picking up your holiday pictures from Boots used to be, but now it's all done via my phone. The wonderful thing about the process is that you can become selective. You certainly don't need to print out every single photo you take, just the ones you love. It's a treat to have a look back through your month in images. I choose around ten from each month – my absolute favourites, the ones that make me smile – and when they arrive, I have a good look through before putting them into one of my neatly labelled photo boxes.

I have photo boxes labelled to cover different periods of my life, and it's an easy and relaxed way to keep them safe and to hand for a quick flick through whenever I want to reminisce. When my dad moved out of the house he lived in with my late mum, I inherited many old photographs. He knew I would want them and, more than that, he trusted me to look after them for my brothers and me to treasure for ever. I labelled some photo boxes 'Oldies', and in they went. For me a strict date order isn't important – it would take the fun away if every time my brothers and I looked through the photos they had to be meticulously replaced in the correct order. No, we rummage and pick out at random, pass piles around, sifting through our wonderful old memories.

Start afresh – don't worry too much about the backlog, otherwise you will be put off starting at all!

If I find a specific section of memories, e.g. a particular holiday, I will pop them in an envelope and write on it within the box.

My Granny would write the date on the back of each photograph she saved. I love this wonderfully organised idea and now do the same – and as I don't print off vast amounts it doesn't take long.

I have simply labelled more recent boxes with the year I start them and, when they are full, I label the end year.

Photos shouldn't be a chore. Never think of organising them as just another task on your action list. If you are going to spend the time getting them in a certain order, then separate the task in your head from anything dull and tedious you have to get done. This is your life and your memories. It's a wonderful and fun project – enjoy spending some time on it.

Magazines

I have many clients and friends who keep magazines for years, then finally become sick of them taking up space and send them straight for recycling, wondering why they kept them in the first place. It just isn't practical to store something that you have already read, or hope to get around to reading, for such a long period of time.

I've noticed that there is often a fear attached to letting magazines go. Perhaps we fear that we will be binning something vital to improving an aspect of our life – that recipe, health piece or parenting article. If you want to save an interesting article, by all means tear it out, and my suggestion would be to store it in an attractive A4 box. This is a box you would keep by your bed or by the sofa for that relaxing time in the evening when you get ten minutes to yourself. Once read, recycle. Start this method with any magazines you buy from now on, but don't be tempted to spend hours going through any existing piles – recycle them and start afresh.

The memory box

Creating a memory box is one of the most special parts of my job, and a real treat for the clients I work with too – this is about collecting together irreplaceable belongings from people's lives that are often scattered around the home and storing them in one safe and secure place. This is where they get to keep all those sentimental items that mean so much to them; items they genuinely couldn't bear to be parted from.

I bought an old vintage white suitcase a few years ago, which I use as my own memory box. (It doesn't have to be a practical, sturdy box – unless you're putting it into long-term storage.) Apparently it had one owner and still contained stamps of her travels inside it. A little piece of history in itself, and the perfect storage item which I don't mind having on view in my spare room. I still get excited looking through my old memories, and the fact that I have been very selective regarding what I have kept over the years means I am not daunted by the thought of pulling this special selection out.

Before clients put an item in a memory box I always

ask them if it would make them smile in ten years' time? And if they would even remember why they had put it in? This often prompts them to reconsider. Memory boxes aren't an excuse to hold on to things to avoid moving them on. Each item you put in should be something that triggers a memory.

Children's memory boxes should be treated with the same consideration. Imagine a scene when your child is older and it is suggested that everyone have a look through their box. If someone is then presented with ten boxes full of old school artwork, piles of scribbles and textbooks, then is this really going to be at all interesting to look back on? I imagine that grown-up child sighing at the thought of trawling through so much stuff!

Now change that scenario to just one or two lighter boxes. Suddenly it's a joy to look through the funny story they wrote at primary school and the picture they drew of your wonderful summer holiday, or a select few baby clothes and perhaps their first pair of shoes. There is no need to keep every single cinema stub, perhaps just their first ever trip. There is no need to keep every exercise book they have ever written in, just an interesting one or two. And it's worth putting a little label on some items with the date: 'your first ever trip to the cinema' or 'these were your first pair of shoes'.

You can store full memory boxes away but keep current ones out and accessible so they are easy to add to. You want to be able to simply post items in them. You could even have smaller ones in the home that fill up and are then emptied into a larger one, stored in the loft. After all, the longer you leave it between look-throughs, the more exciting it is.

Store any clothing you are keeping in acid-free tissue and always use chemical-free moth repellents in your neatly sealed boxes. They could be untouched for a while.

Looking through memories should be a total joy, not an effort.

Living space: general tips

Sofa beds

These have come such a long way since the bulky, uncomfortable ranges in limited designs that used to put people off. Investing in a good sofa bed is an easy way to create an instant spare room.

Wall beds/Murphy beds

When I was little, while my dad was building us a small house in Devon, we lived in a caravan in the garden. My bed was a pull-down one in the main lounge area – I loved it! Ever since those cosy caravan days, I have sworn that one day I'll invest in one – the perfect addition to my spare room/office. I'm totally obsessed with them and the designs on the market are fantastic – it's one of the best space-saving features a home can have.

Coffee table/chest

If you are short of storage space, as most of us are, then using some kind of chest as your coffee table is a great way of doubling up. Use the chest to store items that are not needed regularly – spare bedding, bulky blankets and so on. It's even a great place for storing your memories.

Nests of tables

A design classic that is also really functional! These are a great way of producing extra surface area when needed.

Everything else . . .

Bathrooms and bathroom products

From that fresh-start shower in the morning to a relaxing bath at the end of the day, our bathrooms can be places of clarity and calm. But when crowded with bottles of half-used lotions and potions they quickly become cluttered, especially as storage space is often limited. Products fester at the back of cupboards or cabinets and shelves are crowded with more make-up than you could ever get through. As always, the situation can be turned around and you can reclaim this room as your sanctuary – just follow my straightforward advice.

Lotions and potions

For many of us there is huge temptation to over-buy toiletries, especially when they are on offer. But this usually means we can't clearly see what we have – so we buy more and the amounts build up. When we have several types of the same product on the go, individual items lose their appeal or simply get forgotten. We bulk-buy so that we have 'spares' of everything – but this is at the expense of space and order. Which do you value more?

No one likes waste, so your first task is to use up all your half-finished products! This can be really enjoyable – you discover products you forgot you had and, best of all, your shelves and other surfaces become visible again. For some this may take a while!

I take so much enjoyment in using something up,

it's like that satisfaction of completing a task. When it's finished I then take equal pleasure in choosing its replacement. I'm entitled to buy myself that new product and I'll appreciate it all the more for having a small collection of only my favourites. Once you have cleared the shelves of half-empty bottles you will enjoy the clarity of the space you have claimed back – keep it that way and set yourself the following rules:

Don't have more than a couple of the same product on the go at once.

Make sure all products are visible and accessible – either by bringing them from the back of the cupboard to the front so that you can see what you have or by storing them neatly in baskets or open-topped boxes.

Be mindful that many toiletries have a use-by date.

Be strict when you shop – don't be tempted by big bulk offers; don't over-buy.

Make-up

When bewitched by the glittery colours and trends of a department store make-up counter, the temptation for many can be too much! With multi-buy offers and freebies thrown in, it can be hard to resist spending, and make-up bags can easily get out of control. Older products get forgotten, fester at the bottom of our make-up drawers, become breeding grounds for bacteria and need to be ditched. Just the thought of smearing something that is likely to be contaminated on our faces and around our eyes should be enough to prompt a make-up cull! Here are my top tips for organising your make-up.

If make-up smells bad or has changed colour, throw it out.

Check expiry dates. The packaging for cosmetics should have an open-tub symbol with a number followed by an 'M'. This is the number of months until expiry from the date the product is opened.

Keep your daily make-up in a basket or bag as near to your mirror as possible – you don't need to be sifting through your entire collection every morning. Cut out choices and simplify.

Keep your evening/occasional make-up in a different box or bag (I use a beautiful, decorative House Doctor box). Delving into this box with all my bolder, braver make-up in it is a real treat when getting ready for a night out.

If you buy in error and have opened the product, pass it on immediately to someone who may like it – it may not suit you, but let them enjoy it before its use-by date. Or better still, donate it to a women's refuge. Women often turn up at these shelters with only the clothes on their backs, so your toiletries would be really appreciated.

Towels

Your bathroom definitely loses its appeal as a sanctuary of calm when there are wet towels strewn over the floor. The towel situation tends to get out of control when you have too many in circulation. As a general rule every person needs two towels, plus a set of spares for when they are in the wash. Limiting households to this amount tends to prompt people to look after, hang up and dry the towels that are in use, instead of raiding the cupboard for a fresh one unnecessarily. Like spare bed linen, towels seem to fall into the 'just in case' category, with many homes having cupboards or shelves full. I make frequent trips to Battersea Dogs Home with bags of unwanted towels – why not check to see if your local animal rescue centre would be glad of your extras? You get to free up some space and a charity benefits, it's win-win.

Laundry

Households with children can quickly find the laundry situation getting out of control too – little ones can single-handedly generate an entire load of washing in one day. Some parents witness more daily outfit changes than the audience at a Madonna concert! As with every element of your home, the key is simplicity. Keep your laundry storage straightforward and stick to a routine with your washing. Here is my advice.

Tackle washing one load at a time – don't keep piling in load after load when there is still a mountain of clean clothes to be sorted and put away. It goes back to starting a task and completing it before you embark on the next one. Drawers will be empty because, instead of putting away the clothes you washed several days ago, you are trying to clear a backlog of dirty laundry. Break it down, one load at a time. Wash, dry, sort and fold.

As soon as possible after drying laundry, sort it and, if it doesn't need ironing – many of my clothes don't, it makes life so much easier – fold it. If you don't have time to put clothes away immediately then put them in a neat pile on the end of the bed in the room in which they belong. Each step counts.

Have baskets for linen in every bedroom (not in spare rooms) and train children to pop their dirty clothes in here instead of leaving them on the floor!

Refer to Chapter Five for advice on decluttering your clothes. The fewer clothes you have, the easier it is to put them away and the more pride you will take in maintaining the sense of order. Putting clothes away neatly into streamlined, organised drawers can give you a real buzz!

When storing bed linen, use a marker pen or similar to mark an S, D or K on the label or a corner that should be left visible when the sheet is folded to indicate, without having to unfold it, whether it is a single, double or king.

Packing for a holiday

For me, a key bonus of a good trip away is limited choice – meaning less to think about! For this reason, I always pack light, taking my simple living style with me wherever I go! Like moving house, but on a smaller scale, there is a lot of stress associated with packing for a break – we worry that we have forgotten something vital and overcompensate by taking with us everything that we can squeeze into our suitcases. When we arrive, the worry of what we have forgotten is replaced with despair over the fact that we have brought too much!

I suggest you rethink the way you view packing. With an organised approach, it can be an exciting part of the lead-up to your trip. And don't forget, with the exception of vital medicines, currency and passports, most items that you forget can be relatively easy to source in another country.

Personally, the most important items in my case are a good book, a bikini and lots of sun cream – anything else that fits in my case is a bonus! A slight exaggeration maybe, but I do want my holiday time to mean having little to worry about, fewer choices to face every day. On holiday, the experience I am about to enjoy is more important to me than whether I am wearing the latest trend. If I hesitate over an item when packing, wondering whether I'll have the courage to wear it, then I generally don't pack it. In fact, that means it usually heads straight to the charity shop. A 2016 survey found that the average woman leaves nearly two-thirds of her suitcase contents unworn. This isn't surprising when, on average, women need around fifty-seven items for a two-week holiday, yet many pack nearer to 150. Does this sound familiar to you? Don't haul around a suitcase full of 'just in case' items – pack light and manageable.

As a PA I used to go away on tour for weeks at a time, and knowing that I had to keep charge of not only my own stuff, but also my boss's, meant that I limited what I packed for myself. I would exist comfortably from a small case – the kind you could class as hand luggage – and I would often save buying toiletries until I was away, knowing I would be gone long enough to use a whole tub of anything I bought.

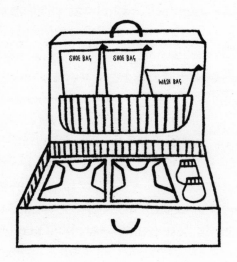

Packing tips

Start with a clear space – a made bed or a clear area of floor.

Keep a master list on your phone or somewhere you will always know to go to. Mine is in the Notes section of my phone and works for every trip I go on – it's just for peace of mind. Make the list detailed so that if time is short, you won't have to waste time thinking.

Pack in outfits for the number of days you are going – lay everything out on your neatly made bed so you have a good view of it all. If you do this, you are less likely to take many extras that you will not need.

If you have followed my steps in Chapter Five you may have a box/area that is designated for items you only wear on your holidays. This makes packing so much easier and straightforward.

Take an absolute minimum of 'just in case'/spare items.

Take toiletries with screw tops – they are much less likely to leak.

Consider where you're going and what you're doing. Does your casual beach holiday really require five pairs of heels?

If travelling with a group then don't double up on electrical items – ask your roomies what they are taking.

Declutter as you go. If you come across an item of holiday wear that hasn't made the cut the last few trips, consider passing it on. There is a reason you're not taking it!

Decant big bottles of shampoo, conditioner and the like into smaller bottles if you do need to save space. Soft bottles are often easier to get the contents out of and use up. If you have any ends of products to use up, here is your perfect opportunity take them – there will be no container to bring home.

Washbags are much simpler to pack when they are cube-like in shape and items easier to find when those washbags are transparent. Mine is always the last thing I pack, so I leave a cube-shaped space to pop it in.

I always take a clean face cloth to lay out make-up on – a habit I learnt from touring days. It can all be rolled away efficiently and packed in your make-up bag.

I stay away from home frequently so I have a spare toiletry bag that is packed ready to go, it contains some miniatures and one of everything I could possibly need – this is easy and efficient.

I've been lucky and have enjoyed many amazing trips over the years, some for pleasure but many for work, making the need for organisation even more vital. Back in the crazy days of being on tour we would sometimes come back and have to be ready to go off again the next day – knowing I could check at a glance I had all I needed was the only way I was going to feel organised and secure. This need for efficiency means I've perfected packing and have confidence that if you follow my advice, it can be enjoyable. For me it means the start of my adventure!

10

Moving House

First things first: let me give you some reassurance. Moving house is often ranked as one of life's most stressful events and although it is, undeniably, a huge upheaval, with good preparation it doesn't have to send your stress levels rocketing!

The stress involved in a move can be fuelled by the fear of change – our homes are our source of stability and leaving them, no matter what the next property offers, can be a wrench. Anxiety over having to leave what is familiar is understandable. It is normal to feel worry and maybe even panic when moving on: these are emotions we may have to accept and ride, but stress brought on by the logistics of the move itself can be avoided – it is within our control to limit this.

Last year alone I helped with more than fifteen house

moves, so I am speaking from experience. I have also moved myself – many times – so I understand the unsettling emotions involved. As with so many changes, the key is in the preparation, and if an organised approach is taken then there is no reason why the process can't be executed in a calm, ordered way.

Obviously there is a lot to do, and usually within the context of an already busy life it may feel like taking on a huge project when you are already operating at full capacity. But, by tackling the workload over a period of time, you really can take so much of the pain out of the process. Try and approach the move as a fresh start – a chance to reboot and make changes. Because it has been labelled by society as 'stressful', it's hard to think outside of that box and flip your mind into what an exciting and positive it this could be. But this is the chance to be energised and empowered. Here you have the opportunity to move on, unhindered by so much baggage, and to press your reset button.

Here are a few tips to help you rise to the challenge of a stress-free move!

Task 1: The moving folder

As soon as you know you are going to be moving, create a moving folder which will contain all the paperwork, notes, lists and details you will need to access easily throughout. Simple and obvious, but this will be your 'go to' so many times in the whole process of moving.

The tasks to be completed in a move can be overwhelming and, in order to prioritise your time, you will need to keep track of what needs to be done and by what deadline. The best way of managing the stress of that extra workload is to keep a list. Often it is not the thought of the individual tasks themselves that provokes anxiety, but the fear of not being able to keep track of what needs doing. I often find offloading everything onto a list has an instant calming effect. But this must be *one list*, in *one notepad*, not several scattered around the place.

Your list will be broken down into three basic sections.

1. Action list

Anything you have to do, from booking cats into kennels to getting someone to pick up unwanted furniture, to booking a removal company and arranging for the cleaners to come in after you've moved out – anything at all that you need to do concerning the move – should be on this list.

2. Rough schedule

This list should have two simple columns – on the left the date and on the right a note of what is happening that day. For example:

DATE	ACTION
Monday 25th July	2pm Estate Agent's Visit 4pm Old furniture Collection
Tuesday 26th July	10am Measure up spaces in new house PACKING DAY
Wednesday 27th July	PACKING DAY
Thursday 28th July	Pack last bits 3pm Collect New house Keys
Friday 29th July	MOVING DAY 8am Removal Men arrive
Saturday 30th July	Unpacking

3. Change-of-details list

In the run-up to your move, as your daily post arrives, add the senders' details to the list of those who you will need to send change-of-address details to – I'm talking about companies and organisations rather than friends and family. Once you have a comprehensive list you can use a website such as iammoving.com to take the hassle out of passing on your new details – make it easy for yourself! It's a simple click-and-send service where you type in your old and new details and it will send a standard 'I am moving' letter to all the relevant companies.

Task 2: The declutter

The lead-up to a move is the perfect time to take a fresh look at the belongings that crowd your home. It makes no sense simply to pack up unwanted clutter and to pay someone to move it into your new house or flat. As soon as you know you are moving, start the process of decluttering – if you have picked up this book purely to read this chapter for advice on moving, then you will need to refer back to Chapters Two and Three for step-by-step guidance on how to reduce the number of possessions in your home.

This is the time to dispense with all the odds and ends that you have accumulated but have no real want or need for. If you are aiming for a decluttered life in your new home, the journey begins before you leave your old one. Departing from one house in a chaotic blur of boxes being filled, transported and unpacked the other end will make it impossible to get into good habits in your new space. Now is the time to discard the trappings of your manic life and allow yourself a new beginning.

Often when I speak to clients, it transpires that the root of the problems in their home often goes back to the manner in which they moved in, even if that was years ago. And when I talk to these people about what went wrong with their house move a common answer is 'It just ended up being such a rush.' Don't let your move fall into the 'last-minute rush' category. Usually we have at least several weeks, often months, to prepare.

Let the decision to move on be your trigger to look at your house and, more importantly, everything in it, with fresh eyes. From that point on, allow extra time in your days and at weekends to get yourself on top of things – pull back on social commitments if you need to, it will be worth it in the end. Make sure that you do not commit yourself to anything around the time that your move is scheduled for. If ever there was a time to practise some strict diary discipline, then this is it!

Some tips to help you stay on top of things . . .

Once you have dates for the move, book as much time off work before and afterwards as you can. If you think you need two days off, take four! People always underestimate how long it takes to unpack properly, and many of my clients who initially unpack in a rush find it affects them for years.

Work day by day, doing little and often. Keep calm and only start a job you can finish that day. Put time aside and stick to it – as I've explained in previous chapters, you don't necessarily have to put whole days aside when decluttering your home, small chunks of time add up. The sooner you start, the more you will get through.

Designate an area of the home that you can live without and use it as a depository for boxes you have packed and for items you have decided to move on.

Always have your recycling, rubbish and charity bags at the ready and get them out of the house as soon as you can.

Task 3: The furniture

If it is possible to gain access to your new home before you move it's a good idea to try and arrange this, to remind yourself of the space in each room. Take photos and measurements to help you plan where furniture will go, think carefully about what will not fit and which new items you might need to purchase. Make sure you take into account the measurements of rooms before getting carried away with ordering new furniture and storage.

Use plans and photos to help you picture what will go where and how the new spaces could work best for you. Any furniture that you know will not fit or suit your new property would be welcomed by charities, many of which offer a collection service. Obviously, these items may be in use right up to the move, so this task is not necessarily about physically moving the items on yet, but it is important to make the arrangements for collection, disposal or resale as soon as possible. In the days around the move you will be grateful to have these details sorted and on your schedule.

Task 4: Packing

Once you have streamlined your possessions to those that you know will have a place in your new (clutter-free!) home, then start packing! If you are packing yourself rather than employing a removal firm to do it, then you are free to start the process whenever suits you – I would advise that this happen as soon as possible. Even if the move is several weeks away, there will be many belongings that you will not need between now and then, so spread the workload and get packing.

Here are my top tips on packing – there's no denying that it is a big task, but the best way to alleviate the anxiety is to get started.

If your removal company does not provide boxes then buy them in bulk, and always order more than you think you will need. Small boxes are an absolute must – you'll always need these most.

Pack ornaments and decorative photographs from all over your home together – they may not work in the same rooms as before. Putting them out is an enjoyable finishing touch at the end of the move.

Clothes that are out of season can be packed long before the move.

If in doubt, pad it out. Use as much paper as needed so the item doesn't break! Use packing paper for breakables, it is easier and quicker to use than bubble wrap.

Don't over-pack and make boxes too heavy. Test the weight as you go.

Put neat labels on boxes rather than scrawling in marker pen. Keep all labels to one area of the box so it's easy to see and refer to – for example, on the top right-hand side of every box label the ROOM the box is going to and the basic CONTENTS. If you have people helping you unload, put corresponding room signs on each door in your new home so there are no mistakes.

Pack yourself an essentials box for the first few hours in your new home – tea, milk, kettle, cups, biscuits. Remember to have enough to cater for whoever is helping you – your workforce will need refuelling! Pack this last so it's off the lorry/van first.

Pack a suitcase for each member of your family, as if they are going on a mini break, containing everything they will need for at least twenty-four hours.

Pack screws and flat-pack stuff in zip-lock bags and stick them to the relevant furniture, and strap remote controls to the back of whatever technology they belong with. Either this, or place them all in one 'useful bits' box.

Task 5: A methodical approach to unpacking

If you have used a removal firm, the chances are your furniture will already be in situ, with a host of boxes around it, hopefully all in the relevant rooms. If you have space to put these boxes to one side this is a great opportunity to look at the room carefully and get a feel for the space.

Enjoy the uncluttered appeal of the room in its current state. Just because you have packed your belongings to bring with you, it doesn't mean that you have to keep them if you feel they will not add anything to the space. Ideally you should have carried out a thorough declutter prior to packing, but unpacking can itself be an opportunity to shed some belongings that may have slipped through the net! Once you start filling furniture and floor space, you may well find yourself leaving several items in their boxes – perhaps they looked right in your last home but don't quite fit in this new space. To be objective in your unpacking you need time. Take care and be methodical.

The biggest mistake people make is wanting to unpack everything quickly to get it all done. The rush is often justified by the intention to 'do it properly later'. Believe me, 'later' rarely comes! This is your chance to get it right. Start as you mean to go on, with clarity and order. Follow my steps for organised unpacking:

If you have children or pets, arrange for them to be taken care of around the time that you move in. You need to be able to focus on the task in hand.

Allocate a space for unpacked boxes and flatten them immediately as they can take up a lot of room. If the boxes were provided by the removal company, make sure you arrange a date for their collection. This will also give you a goal to work towards.

Commit to a room and do not get distracted by other areas – when you have a whole house to tackle it is easy to flit from one room to another without putting anything away properly.

Have a charity box ready for those items that you feel don't belong in your new home.

Empty out the contents of each box on to a clear surface – don't put them straight into their new home. For example, don't be tempted to start piling your kitchen utensils straight into a kitchen drawer only to find that the drawer isn't quite big enough to hold them all. Assess exactly what you have before you choose its home.

To recap:

Good luck in your adventure in your exciting new home! Here is a summary of my advice to make this move a success.

Start soon. Once you know that you will be moving, create a folder for all the relevant paperwork and a list broken down into three sections: action, schedule, change-of-address details.

Declutter like never before! Seize the chance to rid yourself of possessions you no longer want or need – it makes no sense to package up unwanted belongings and cart them to a new home. This is your chance for a fresh start.

Work out what furniture you will be taking with you and arrange for the rest to be disposed of or recycled.

Get packing! Start as soon as possible. Order more boxes than you think you'll need, especially smaller ones which always come in really useful. Be methodical, mark boxes clearly, using labels on which you should write what their rough contents are and which room they will be going in.

Take your time unpacking. The end is in sight, but do not rush this final challenge. Unpacking in a methodical way will set you up for organised living in the years ahead, so allocate more time than you think it will take.

And one last tip – accept offers of help! Have a think about what other people could do for you over the coming weeks to make life easier. That way, if anyone offers, you can be ready with a suggestion of how they could help out: it could be anything from having the kids over, to preparing a meal that you can heat up easily on you first night in your new home.

Don't be daunted by what is ahead: a calm, organised house move can be achieved by breaking the job down, I've seen it done many times!

Conclusion

You've read the theories and the real-life accounts about how my methods not only work, but make a massive impact on lives – now it is within your power to do this!

Start small, ideally, as I suggest, with your sock drawer, and feel the difference you can make to a small area. Then imagine applying this level of organisation to your entire home. There is no need to live in fear of what might lurk at the back of the cupboard or to despair over lost belongings . . . it's time to leave those days behind.

From reading about my methods you will know that nothing I suggest is rocket science, I have not tried to baffle you with complex systems. I have implemented all of my methods hundreds of times over the last fifteen years or so. And because my techniques make so much sense, incorporating them into your daily life will be almost effortless. Decluttering does not have to be an overwhelming, stressful task with strict rules to follow. 'Habits are formed when they are easy to do', says Dr Steve Peters in his ground-breaking study of the human mind, *The Chimp*

Paradox, and I believe this is especially true when it comes to getting into good habits around your home.

Writing this book has reminded me of so many satisfying moments when, from chaos and despair, I have worked with a client to bring calmness and serenity to their home. Often they have put the task off for months, even years, and when they enjoy their new-found space they tell me they wish they'd tackled it sooner.

In so many areas of our lives it's easier to conjure up excuses for not solving a problem rather than to get stuck in and tackle it head-on. Decluttering needn't be the giant task that you cannot face or that you feel you don't have time for. I've made it easy for you to tackle small areas at a time, and to break jobs down into manageable chunks. Remind yourself that perfection is never the end goal, don't overthink it – just do it!

You not only deserve, but *need* a place of calm and order in your life, in which to start your busy day and to come home to. We all have our wobbles along the way but, believe me, dealing with life's ups and downs is much more manageable when you have order on the home front. Life is demanding and we don't need clutter to cloud our judgement and crowd our homes, we need space to think and breathe.

And now it's over to you, everything you need to know is here to help you bring clarity into your home, and therefore, into your life – good luck, and enjoy the journey!

Vicky

xxx

Vicky's Recommended Suppliers

Hangers
www.youneedavicky.com/shop

Drawer dividers
www.theholdingcompany.co.uk

CDs
www.musicmagpie.co.uk

Photos
www.photobox.co.uk
www.lalalab.com

Under-bed storage boxes
www.argos.co.uk
www.theholdingcompany.co.uk
www.thewhitecompany.com
www.ikea.com

Bisley filing cabinets

www.ryman.co.uk or search for Bisley 5-, 10- or 15-drawer cabinets

Wall beds

www.clei.co.uk

Chemical-free products

www.methodproducts.co.uk

uk.ecover.com

Memory boxes (by Bigso)

www.theholdingcompany.co.uk

Baskets

Some of the most beautiful baskets I have seen are in Zara Home, Homebase and The White Company

Vicky's List of Charities for Donations

Make-up and toiletries
Give and MakeUp
http://www.carolinehirons.com/p/give-and-makeup.html

Animal rescue homes
Many accept towels which they can find so much use for. Get in touch with them first, to check

Hospitals and care homes
Check if they need their libraries refreshing with new books

Hoarding
There are specialist charities to assist with Hoarding. Websites such as those below offer support for this condition:

www.hoardinguk.org
www.helpforhoarders.co.uk
www.mind.org.uk

Food Banks

Food banks work to feed and support those in need. With hundreds of locations across the UK and internationally there are many you can choose from but I love the Trussell Trust (www.trusselltrust.org). Foods you can donate include:

Meals in a can (stew, chilli, soup)

Tuna and canned meat

Peanut Butter

Canned foods with pop-top lids

Low-sugar cereals

100% fruit juices in single serving boxes

Canned fruit packed in juice

Canned vegetables (low salt)

Specific charities

Charity shops may vary in what they take so call to check in advance if it's an unusual item. Most shops will collect on request, depending on area, availability and items – again, call in advance if you're not sure

Age UK

www.ageuk.org.uk

All Age UK shops have donation bins for mobile phones and foreign currency

Small electrical goods can be taken to their shops if they are fully working

Furniture items cannot be taken in standard shops, but there are specialised furniture shops you can get in touch with

All clothes, accessories and bric-a-brac, cutlery, plates

Clothing that is unsaleable can be sent for rags, which means the charity still receives money for it

DVDs, CDs and books

Children's toys

No linen

Age UK also recommend a service for recycling your old laptops and mobiles securely, with an easy-to-follow online service: https://www.rdc-cbs.com/partner/ageuk

Barnardo's
www.barnardos.org.uk

Women's, men's and children's clothing

Shoes, handbags, jewellery and accessories

Quality homeware – from vases and photo frames to ornaments and tea sets

Furniture (selected furniture shops only)

Electrical goods

Books, toys, CDs and DVDs

Mobile phones

Foreign currency

British Heart Foundation
www.bhf.org.uk

Clothes

Furniture

Electricals

Shoes, handbags, jewellery

DVDs, CDs, vinyls and books

Bric-a-brac

Children's toys

British Red Cross

www.redcross.org.uk

Clothing

They also welcome any old clothes or textiles that are no longer usable, as they can still raise money from them by selling to textile merchants

Footwear, handbags, non-pierced jewellery, belts

Homeware sets – cooking and dining

Soft furnishings including cushion covers, curtains and linen

DVDs, CDs, vinyls and books

Gift items

New boxed electrical items

Some shops accept second-hand furniture

Cancer Research

www.cancerresearchuk.org

Women's, men's and children's clothing

Accessories including shoes, belts, handbags and jewellery

Quality homeware – anything from cushions to crockery

Linens

Books, CVs and DVDs

Mobile phones and used printer cartridges

Electricals (please check with your local shop before you donate these)

CLIC Sargent

www.clicsargent.org.uk

Clothing including retro, vintage and bridal

Jewellery and accessories

Collectables – they have an award-winning ebay shop

DVDs, CDs and books

Bric-a-brac

China and glassware

Household textiles

Musical instruments and sheet music

Laptops, mobile phone handsets, cameras, IT equipment and printer cartridges

Marie Curie

They say they especially love:

Women's clothing and accessories

Shoes – all kinds

DVDs, CDs and books (check with your nearest store)

Mary's Living and Giving

www.savethechildren.org/get-involved/
charity-shopping/marys-living-and-giving

Clothing (women's, men's and children's)

Homeware

Accessories

Artwork

Limited Edition Books

Footwear

Cards

Mind

www.mind.org.uk

Clothing and accessories

Homeware

Linens

DVDs, CDs and books

Children's games and toys

Furniture, white goods and electrical – specialist Mind shops will take, but call and check locations

Octavia Foundation

www.octaviafoundation.org.uk

Clothing, footwear and accessories

Jewellery

DVDs, CDs and books

Small electrical items

Oxfam

www.oxfam.org.uk

Good-quality clean clothing and shoes including retro,

vintage, bridal and even bras!

Bags and accessories

DVDs, CDs and books

Musical instruments and sheet music

Homewares including kitchenware and ornaments, pictures and collectables

Soft furnishings – linen, curtains, knitted items and blankets

Mobile phones

Furniture

Stamps and coins

Princess Alice Hospice

www.pah.org.uk

Clothing (women's, men's and children's)

Bridal

Accessories

Homewares

Furniture (collection service from your home can be arranged)

Please note some shops specialise in furniture so please check with your local shop

Royal Trinity Hospice

https://www.royaltrinityhospice.london

Clothing, shoes and accessories

Bed Linen

Curtains

Homewares

Small electrical items (in working condition)

Books

RSPCA

www.rspca.org.uk

Clothing (women's, men's and children's)

Shoes

Accessories including jewellery and bags

Bedlinen (no quilts or pillows)

Small electricals

Books

DVDs & CDs

Bric-a-Brac

The RSPCA does not accept any fur, feather or fishing products

Salvation Army

www.salvationarmy.org.uk

Clothing

Shoes (paired)

Accessories

Household Items

Books

No large furniture, electricals, videos or casettes

Scope
www.scope.org.uk

Clothing

Shoes

Accessories

Books

DVDs and CDs

Bric-A-brac

Sense
https://www.sense.org.uk

Clothing (fashion & retro styles)

Handbags, shoes and accessories

Jewellery (costume and genuine styles)

Antiques and collectables

Household items (including linen)

Furniture

Electrical Goods

Books

CDs, cassette tapes, records and singles

DVDs and videos

Toys and games

Bric-a-brac

Foreign and pre-decimal currency

Clean carrier bags

Shelter

www.shelter.org.uk

Clothing (women's, men's and children's and including vintage items)

Bric-a-brac

Books

CDs, records, videos

Electrical items are received by Shelter through SHP limited who recycle them

Sue Ryder

www.sueryder.org

Bicycles (check with your local shop before arriving)

Furniture

Dolls Houses

Clothing

Accessories

Shoes

Electricals

Books

Records, CDs and DVDs

Guitars

Traid

www.traid.org.uk

Clothes (womens, men's and children's – all styles wanted including designer, high street and vintage)

Shoes (paired)

Accessories (bags, scarves, jewellery, hats etc)

Linen (e.g. curtains)

Books and music

Homeware (of all kinds)

Will collect clothes if you have at least one large bin liner full

YMCA

www.ymca.org.uk

Clothing

Shoes

Accessories

Books

CDs and DVDs

Household linen

Bric-a-brac

Will collect furniture and electrical items

References

Bourg Carter, Sherrie, *High Octane Women: How Superachievers Can Avoid Burnout*, Prometheus, 2010

Coughlan, Sean, 'UK families face consumer pressure', BBC news, September 2011 (http://www.bbc.co.uk/news/education-14898614)

Flett, Gordon L.; Hewitt, Paul L.; Heisel, Marnin J., 'The destructiveness of perfectionism revisited: Implications for the assessment of suicide risk and the prevention of suicide', *Review of General Psychology*, Vol 18(3), September 2014, 156–72. (http://psycnet.apa.org/index.cfm?fa=buy.optionToBuy&id=2014-38880-002)

Kambolis, Michele, *Generation Stressed*, Lifetree Media, 2014

London, Bianca, 'Women over-pack by TWO THIRDS when they go on holiday', *Mail Online*, 8 August 2013 (http://www.dailymail.co.uk/femail/article-2386742/Women-pack-by-TWO-THIRDS-holiday-packing-150-items.html#ixzz4CL58vRqi)

Payne, Kim John, *Simplicity Parenting*, Ballantine, 2010

Sarda-Joshi, Gauri, 'Researchers have identified a series of psychological changes that occur when we wear certain clothes' (http://brainfodder.org/psychology-clothes-enclothed-cognition/)

Saxbe, Darby E. and Repetti, Rena, 'No place like home: home tours correlate with daily patterns of mood and cortisol', *Personality and Social Psychology Bulletin*, 2010. (http://www.celf.ucla.edu/2010_conference_articles/ Saxbe_Repetti_2010b.pdf)

Scot, Ellen, 'Sleeping in a messy room might be ruining your sleep', Metro.co.uk, 20 June 2015 (http://metro. co.uk/2015/06/20/sleeping-in-a-messy-room-might-be-ruining-your-sleep-5255644/)

Seldin, Tim, 'Children are Little Scientists: Encouraging Discovery Plan' (https://childdevelopmentinfo.com/ child-development/play-work-of-children/ children-little-scientists/)

Selhub, Dr Eva, *Your Health Destiny: How to Unlock Your Natural Ability to Overcome Illness, Feel Better, and Live Longer*, HarperCollins, 2015

Acknowledgements

Emma Cooling

I have looked up to my cousin Emma since I was a little girl. In my eyes she was clever, beautiful inside and out and inspiring – and she still is. She not only juggles a busy life with three amazing little boys but is the pillar of her community, an amazing wife, sister, daughter and for me the best cousin in the world. When it came to the task of writing a book there was never a question of who would help me. It was only ever going to be her. She knows me and she translates my thoughts and words like no one else could.

Thank you so much, Emma. This book would definitely not have been possible if it wasn't for you.

The Boys

My fantastic big brothers Nick and Jamie, who I describe as 'organisationally challenged', inspire me to make systems simple. If it works for them it can work for anyone! Thanks for always supporting everything I have ever done and having my back no matter what. I love you both so much.

Mum and Dad

My brothers and I referred to Mum and Dad as 'Mumbo' and 'Pa' – and they were the most amazing team you could know. Mum passed away in 2013 and Dad chose to live on and find his second chance at happiness – just as Mum asked him to. Now he and his new wife Ying live for experiences . . . every day is a great day. I couldn't be prouder.

My Friends

My rocks . . . my utter rocks through everything. The love I feel for them all simply can't be described in words – not without more help from Cousin Emma's writing skills anyway!

My Team

Who would have thought there would be a profession which I truly love so much? It still makes me feel lucky every single day. The people I work with not only make it possible but make it fun. To everyone who has worked with me, past and present, thank you so much for all of your hard work and support.

Polly, Vicki, Shelly, Allison, Becca, Jenna, Lucy, Alicia, Katie, Joanne, Sian, Georgie, Kelly and Kat.

Nikki Johnceline managed to get me press coverage when I first started out, despite my profession being relatively unheard of in the UK. Thanks for your faith in me and my little business. It did and does mean the world to me.

My dear friends Alex Davison and Lindsey Evans – both

PR experts who have helped me since day one, advising me on anything and everything at the drop of a hat. I can't thank you enough for all of your time and care.

Polly Hadden-Paton – from the second I met you I knew I would know you forever! A best friend, a business partner and the one who 'gets it' more than anyone.

Little, Brown
Ideas that I have been shouting about for years being made into a book … Wow. I can still hardly believe it. I can't believe it's written. Thanks for your belief in me and for your enthusiasm on the subject I am so passionate about.

Thanks Hannah Boursnell, Rhiannon Smith, Clara Diaz and Justine Gold – you are the BEST. And thank you to Debbie Powell for the beautiful illustrations – you've brought my book to life!